ORSON WELLES
AND
ROGER HILL:
A FRIENDSHIP IN THREE ACTS

"THE ONLY REAL EXISTENCE WE HAVE
IS THE PEOPLE WE LOVE"

BY TODD TARBOX

ORSON WELLES AND ROGER HILL:
A FRIENDSHIP IN THREE ACTS
©2013 TODD TARBOX

Published in the USA by:

BEARMANOR MEDIA
P.O. BOX 71426
ALBANY, GEORGIA 31708
www.BearManorMedia.com

ISBN-10: 1-59393-260-X (alk. paper)
ISBN-13: 978-1-59393-260-2 (alk. paper)

DESIGN AND LAYOUT: VALERIE THOMPSON

No one had ever engaged in a dull conversation with Orson Welles. Exasperating, yes; sometimes eruptive, unreasonable, ferocious, and convulsive... yet eloquent, penetrating, exciting, and always, never failingly always—even at the sacrifice of accuracy and his own vanity—witty and never, never, never, dull.

—JOSEPH COTTEN

Many people will walk in and out of your life, but only true friends will leave footprints in your heart.

—ELEANOR ROOSEVELT

But if the while I think on thee, dear friend,
All losses are restor'd, and sorrows end.

—WILLIAM SHAKESPEARE, FROM SONNET XXX

CHARACTERS

ORSON WELLES

ROGER HILL

TABLE OF CONTENTS

IN MEMORY OF HASCY TARBOX, TODD'S OTHER GENIUS,* ORSON'S PEER AND MY PEERLESS FATHER (1918–1991)

Hascy Tarbox, 1936

* "'There is this boy, Hascy Tarbox,' Orson tells me... unaware that I have already met him—although to my eyes Hascy Tarbox is hardly a boy, but a distinguished, silver-haired grandfather in his sixties. (But to Orson's eyes—and this is key to comprehending him—Hascy is still a boy, still Todd's other genius, with whom he is in competition for Skipper's love and respect.) 'There is this boy, Hascy Tarbox, who was younger than I... and became a commercial artist and a cartoonist—with a lot of talent... He could have gone out into the great world and made a big success, but he stayed and married one of Roger's daughters and adores Roger... he's the one who gave up the world career to be near Roger.'"

From *Orson Welles: a Biography* by Barbara Leaming

FOREWORD

I found *Orson Welles and Roger Hill: A Friendship in Three Acts* fascinating, touching, and revealing of Orson and Roger. It certainly is the Orson I knew in all his complexity and brilliance.

—PETER BOGDANOVICH, American film historian, director,
writer, actor, producer, critic, and
author of *This is Orson Welles*

I read *A Friendship in Three Acts* with absolute delight. At last I have got what I have been looking for in vain till now: the sound of Welles's private voice, the warmth, easiness, modesty, fantasy of which so many have spoken but which none have been able to reproduce. Here it is at last, along with the moving revelation of the depth of feeling between Orson Welles and Roger Hill: the undeviating, unconditional but intelligent love in which Orson clearly rejoices, and by which he is so evidently sustained, even through the worst reverses and most bitter disappointments.

A Friendship in Three Acts is an essential document for an understanding of Welles. Even for those without a professional fascination with the man, it is a rich and engaging read, a real dialogue between two remarkable men.

—SIMON CALLOW, English actor, writer, director, and author
of *Orson Welles: The Road to Xanadu*,
and *Orson Welles: Hello Americans*, the first
two of an eventual three-volume Welles
biography.

The major and longest-lasting close friendship of Orson Welles's life was with one of his earliest role models—his teacher, advisor, and theatrical mentor at the Todd School who later became the school's headmaster, Roger Hill. Hill's grandson, Todd Tarbox, has given us invaluable and candidly intimate glimpses into many of its stages, especially ones towards the beginning and end of that diverse and complicated saga. In the process, he also confounds and complicates the array of "weak" and flawed father figures that populate most of Welles's films, all the way from *Citizen Kane* and *The Magnificent Ambersons* through *The Trial, Chimes at Midnight, Don Quixote,* and *The Other Side of the Wind,* with a bracing and ennobling alternative to that pattern, an unwavering relationship of mutual admiration and respect that was a clear source of strength to both of them. The portrait that emerges is not only one of Welles that is revised and corrected from the more mythical versions that we have of him, but also a look at Hill himself that is multifaceted, sturdy, and highly charismatic.

—JONATHAN ROSENBAUM, American film critic and author,
whose books include *Movies as Politics, Moving Places: A Life in the Movies,* and *Discovering Orson Welles.* Additionally, he edited Orson Welles and Peter Bogdanovich's book, *This is Orson Welles.*

Introduction

*O*rson Welles & Roger Hill: A Friendship in Three Acts chronicles the seven-decade relationship between Orson Welles and his mentor and treasured friend, my grandfather, Roger Hill. Orson's attachment to my grandfather was instant, reciprocal, and developed into an enduring love. Their intimate conversations, at times frothy and at other times solemn, reflect their incalculable interests and abiding fascination with the human comedy.

Two years after the death of his mother, Beatrice, Orson was enrolled at the Todd School for Boys in Woodstock, Illinois, where Roger Hill was a teacher, and son of the headmaster, Noble Hill.

Orson arrived at Todd on September 15, 1926. He was eleven years old. Orson, like all entering students, was given the Stanford-Binet test measuring intelligence, consisting of questions followed by multiple answers, requiring the student to underscore the correct response. Orson's first test had this question: "Deserts are crossed by horses, trains, automobiles, camels, donkeys." Orson underscored every item and wrote "See other side." On the back of the test he wrote, "All of these, but the writer was obviously too dumb to know it." This and subsequent annual tests established Orson's IQ at 185; 140 and above was considered the genius level.

During Orson's five years at Todd, he literally and figuratively found his voice writing, designing, directing, and acting in myriad theatrical productions. In May 1931, Orson and his classmates graduated after their sophomore year. My grandfather, who succeeded his father as headmaster, expanded Todd to four years of high school shortly after Orson received his diploma. The culmination of Orson's acting career at Todd was his successful amalgam of Shakespeare's

English history plays, *Five Kings*, which was performed at graduation. Eight years later, he expanded his creation and staged it as a Theatre Guild/Mercury Theatre production, and in 1966, transformed it into one of his most memorable films, *Chimes at Midnight*.

Another project Orson directed while simultaneously producing and acting in *Five Kings* was fashioning the following year's school catalog, *Todd: A Community Devoted to Boys and Their Interests*. The fifteen-year-old polymath portrayed Todd to prospective students and parents with a crystalline eye and an affectionate heart:

> Todd is not perfect. This we realized and this we rejoiced in, for if it were, the joy of making it finer would be gone... Our school is the oldest in the west. It was started in 1848 by Richard Todd. He had a wife whose name was Martha Clover and her mother's name was Wallingford, and that is where we get the names of some of our buildings. Mr. Todd came from Princeton.

Richard Kimball Todd, 1890

Noble Hill, 1890

Noble Hill was in charge for forty years. He enlarged the campus to about ten times its old size and added the forty acre north campus.

Roger Hill, 1936

Roger Hill, or Skipper as everybody calls him, has been here twelve years and everybody knows what he has done...

Todd is a bustling bee hive of activity from dawn until dark and, for some of us, on into the night. Skipper tells us there is no joy compared with having accomplished something worthwhile with your hands or your brain and we have found he's right.

Every boy can express himself in some line of useful or artistic endeavor, and the program at Todd is to give him this opportunity. In the next few pages, we will try to give you some slight picture of this guild of young artists and artisans who are finding the thrill there is in doing the work of the world and who have learned that usefulness is the highest good and greatest joy.

Reflecting on Todd dramatics, Orson wrote:

Todd Dramatics is the activity that touches every boy here and gives him a chance to express any talent he has. It is not a single activity, but a combination of all. The theatre blends in a common art the talents of the story teller, the poet, the speaker, the singer, the dancer, the composer, the mimic, the artist, the carpenter, and the electrician.

The Todd Troupers are the main school dramatic organization. They are well known in Chicago and Northern Illinois and have won many prizes in Chicago drama contests. The other dramatic clubs that give productions for outsiders are the Junior Troupers, the Lean Pigeons, and the Tiny Troupers. Two independent clubs have been organized by the boys themselves to give Saturday night entertainments after the movies. One is the Slap Stick Club and the other, the Paint and Powder Club.

The Troupers and Junior Troupers have a regular subscription season in our theater and stage about six plays a year, including an annual musical comedy. Some of the productions are taken to theaters in other towns if the scenery is not too elaborate to move. The scenery is in every case original, being designed and built and painted by the boys. The make-ups are also done by the boys. Our stage is completely equipped. The lighting is most modern with all of the circuits on dimmers, and a plaster back wall similar to the Goodman's in Chicago makes possible very realistic and stunning outdoor effects.

There is an arras or drape setting for simple plays but these drapes can be removed and solid scenery used. The rigging loft is equipped with ten sets of lines for hanging drops. A stairway back stage leads to our dressing rooms and large costume and property rooms where hundreds of costumes are stored. About half of the plays are original and the musical comedy is always original with some help from the faculty....

Orson's cover illustration of *Todd: A Community Devoted to Boys and Their Interests*

Determined to bypass college and leap from being a student to becoming a professional actor, in the month he graduated from Todd, Orson placed an ad in the "At Liberty Dramatic Artists" column of *Billboard* magazine:

ORSON WELLES—Stock, Characters, Heavies, Juveniles or as cast. Also specialties, chalk talk or can handle stage. Young, excellent appearance, quick sure study. Lots of pep, experience and ability. Want place in good stock company for remainder of season. Photos on request. Address ORSON WELLES c/o H.L. Powers, Illinois Theatre, 65 E. Jackson Blvd., Chicago, Ill.

His spirited, self-confident notice was met with weeks of silence, which prompted him to run a second, more enticing notice a month later:

Orson Welles is willing to invest modest amount of cash and own services as Heavy, Character, and Juvenile in good summer stock or repertory production. Reply to Orson Welles, Dramatic Coach, Todd Seminary for Boys, Woodstock, Illinois.

The second submission was no more successful than the first, much to the delight of his guardian, Dr. Maurice Bernstein, whom Welles called "Dadda," who favored Orson furthering his education in the halls of academe and not in front of playhouse footlights. With no professional acting offers, Orson opted to pursue temporarily another of his gifts: art. He enrolled in a summer class at the Art Institute of Chicago taught by the noted Russian émigré stage designer, Boris Anisfeldt. Welles found Anisfeldt fascinating, but Orson had a distaste for being "incarcerated in a classroom." An unquenchable lifelong wanderlust, coupled with a severe bout of hay fever, drove Orson to escape the classroom and the hay fever of the Middle Border by convincing Bernstein, after much inveigling, to allow him to travel to the British Isles on a painting tour, with the understanding that at the end of his travels, Orson would enroll at a university.

In August, recounting his good fortune to Skipper, Orson wrote:

Three days of particularly vicious domestic warfare… ended in a roundtable conference which found all the principal powers as determined as ever. Dadda had thought the matter over and decided he could not permit my having ought to do with the diseased and despicable theatre. The deuteragonist and the tritagonist questioned the educational value and the chorus (everybody about) was uniformly and maddeningly derisive. Things went from bad to worse. Alternately I defended and offended. My head remained bloody but unbowed and my nose, thanks to the thoughtful blooming of some neighboring clover (which I assured the enemy was ragweed!) began to sniffle hay-feverishly, and the household was illusioned into the realization that something had to be done.

It was then that Dadda arrived at a momentous decision—and in the spirit of true martyrdom chose the less of two great evils. Going abroad alone is not quite as unthinkable as joining the theatre—and so… I was whisked out of the fire into the frying pan. Four days later I was in New York!

A few months of walking and painting in Ireland and Scotland… and then on to England where there are schools—and theatres!!!!!!

"Theatres" is the operative word. Not long after procuring a donkey cart and for several weeks painting his way through County Donegal, he landed at the Gate Theatre in Dublin, headed by co-directors Hilton Edwards and Micheál mac Liammóir. In mac Liammóir's book *All for Hecuba*, written twenty years after first encountering young Orson, he describes Welles's indelible introduction:

Hilton walked into the scene dock one day and said, 'Somebody strange has arrived from America; come and see what you think: tall, and young, fat. Says he's been with the Theatre Guild in New York. I don't believe a word of it but he's interesting. I think we should give him an audition…'

I found, as he had hinted, a very tall young man with a chubby face, full powerful lips and disconcerting Chinese eyes. His hands were very beautifully shaped. The voice, with its brazen transatlantic sonority, was already that of a preacher, a leader, a man of power;

it bloomed and blossomed its way through the dusty air of the scene dock as though it would crush down walls and rip up the floor. He moved in a leisurely manner from foot to foot and surveyed us with magnificent patience as though here was our chance to do something beautiful at last. Were we going to take it? Well, just too bad for us if we let the moment slip. And all this did not come from mere youth but from some ageless and inner confidence that no one could blow out. It was unquenchable. That was his secret. He knew that he was precisely what he himself would have chosen to be had God consulted him on the subject at his birth. Whether we and the world felt the same—well, that was for us to decide.

They quickly decided "to take" what Orson had to offer, hiring him initially as a scene painter and publicity assistant, which within days evolved into being cast to play the part of Duke Karl Alexander of Württemberg in *Jew Süss*.

The ink had hardly dried on *Todd: A Community Devoted to Boys and Their Interests* when Orson, writing wistfully from Ireland, requested Skipper send him a copy and added, "I am unspeakably lonesome for Todd—which is just another way of spelling your name." The resilient tie with my grandfather, unlike many of Orson's other relationships, never waned.

While championing Orson's desire to pursue the theatre, my grandfather believed that time spent honing his craft at an institution of higher learning was an option Orson should consider.

To provide Orson such a choice, Skipper wrote to Clyde Tull, an English professor at Cornell College, who had established the school's theatre program, and when not teaching, toured on the Chautauqua circuit with his playwright wife, Jewel:

Professor Clyde Tull
Cornell College
Mount Vernon, Iowa
September 6, 1931

Dear Professor Tull:

I am writing you about one of our graduates, Orson Welles. He was really doing post graduate work with us last year and I am anxious to have him located for his best interest this fall.

You may have heard of him. Nearly everyone connected with the arts, the opera, or the stage in Chicago knows him and they have all done their best to spoil him, but I think he is very sound and very sensible, although he is definitely talented to the point of genius.

He has been offered a scholarship by the Harvard Drama School next year, but I feel that this should be postponed at least two years. Fritz Lieber wants him in his company and well he might, for I consider him better than anyone of them.

His mother and father are dead; his guardian is Dr. Maurice Bernstein, a well-known Chicago orthopedist but probably better known just now through the newspaper publicity in regard to his divorce from his prima donna wife, Edith Mason.

Although up to this summer he has done little with his artistic talents, they are equal to his dramatic ones and both the Doctor and I are hoping that he will follow these for a life work. This summer, Anisfeldt, the Russian scene designer who is now a guest teacher at the Art Institute [of Chicago], took him under his wing, and wants him to live with him this winter and study art, but I would rather have him out of the city.

The last half of this summer, he has been in Ireland. Each summer for several years, he has taken a somewhat similar trip; last summer to China, the summer before to Central Europe. I am enclosing my most recent letter from him and also a copy of our school catalog. Every word of this book was either written or edited by him. The only "cheating" I did in this was to make him cut out some of his best bits of writing as they were too completely mature. . . .

I have been told of your work and I am writing to you rather than to some vague official of your institution as I know his case is one that will interest you greatly. He will be back in New York in about a week and I should like to have him definitely entered in Cornell by that time. Please let me know at once just what steps I should take toward this.

Thanking you for your cooperation in this and assuring you that you have a treat in store for you if the lad comes to Cornell. I am

Sincerely yours,
Roger Hill

Skipper's effort proved feckless. Orson wasn't interested in Cornell and its dramaturgy department. He knew that neither could satiate his vast talent and ambition. Only the world stage was big enough to hold and satisfy both.

Living in Europe in the early '50s, nomadic Orson was asked in an interview where he considered home. After an extended pause he replied, "I have lots of homes …but, I suppose it's Woodstock, Illinois if it's anywhere. I went to school there for five years, and if I think of home, it's there. It may be a tedious bromide to say that school days are the happiest days of your life, but Roger Hill and his staff were so unique, and the school so imbued with real happiness, that one could hardly fail to enjoy oneself within its boundaries."

Orson's visits home to the Hills, and the extended Todd family were frequent from the time he graduated until the school closed. On one homecoming, after delivering a speech, *Moral Indebtedness*, on November 11, 1943 at the Chicago Stadium on behalf of the United Nations Committee to Win the Peace, he and his bride of two months, Rita Hayworth, spent several days at Todd. After a dinner party hosted by my parents at their campus cottage, in a guest book extended by my mother, Orson wrote effusively:

Dear Happy Family.

"Just a cottage small."
"Just a little love nest."
"My Blue Heaven."

"A newly wedded husband salutes you."

These and a thousand more are the ballads of an American dream. They are part of an immemorial cliché concealing an enormous truth. You are the joyful participants in that truth. You are its celebrants. You have shattered the platitudes and enshrined a mystery older than roofs. A newly wedded husband salutes you.

Ever,
Orson
P.S. The sponge cake was just gorgeous!

One of Orson's frequent visits to Todd was in 1948 when the school celebrated its 100th anniversary. English teacher Pat Armstrong is seated at his right; a pensive Roger Hill is on his left.

Much is known about the fabulous Orson Welles, to cite the title of Peter Noble's 1956 biography. Comparatively little is known about Roger Edward Hill, who for thirty years was the headmaster of the Todd School for Boys, and known by all in his orbit as "Skipper," in tribute to his passion for sailing.

Skipper was born in 1895, twenty years to the month Orson's senior. He outlived his stellar student and friend by five years. As a child, Skipper attended his father's school, known when he was a boy and when Orson attended, as the Todd Seminary for Boys. He was Noble and Grace Rogers Hill's second child, their first being a daughter, Carol. His adored and adoring mother, referred to on campus as "the Mother of Boys" died on the school's commencement day, June 11, 1914. His formidable father, Noble, died in May of 1953, just before his ninety-fifth birthday.

After graduating from Todd, Skipper attended the University of Illinois, where he met his future wife, Hortense Gettys. They were married and moved to Chicago where my grandfather began a career in advertising working as a copywriter at Montgomery Ward. While Skipper was at Ward's, Noble importuned his son to jettison "the world of puffery," and return to Woodstock where he and my grandmother would join the Todd faculty. They accepted Noble's

"The Mother of Boys"

Dear queen of all hearts, sweet mother of boys,
Whose whole life was lived for others,
Who daily performed without trumpet or noise
The work of a score of mothers.

She lived for her boys through long, long years,
Giving love in unstinted measure,
Entered into their joys, their hopes and fears,
Their interests her only pleasure.

In this life of service time never was found
For pursuit of the common joys,
And her rich reward is at last to be crowned
The beautiful "Mother of Boys."
                                    NOBLE HILL

GRACE ROGERS HILL

Todd Seminary for Boys, Woodstock-Illinois

A poem by Noble Hill in memory of his wife, Grace Rogers Hill, Todd School's "Mother of Boys"

offer with alacrity, and made Todd School their home until the school closed in 1954.

In 1929, Noble deeded the school to Skipper, and retired with his second wife, Nellie Rathbone, a widowed cousin of Grace, to Ventura, California.

During his tenure as headmaster at Todd, Skipper fashioned one of the most progressive educational programs in the country. His educational philosophy embraced the concept that all youngsters were "created creators." Toward that end, Todd offered an extra-curricular program that was generations ahead of its time. It included producing sound motion pictures and theatrical productions. Two buses, referred to as "Big Berthas," permitted students and faculty to travel throughout the United States, Canada, and Mexico. Crewed by the Todd faculty and students, the school's schooner, *Sea Hawk*, cruised the Great Lakes. A 300-acre working farm, run in large measure by students, expanded their appreciation of agronomy and enhanced the school's cuisine. Todd maintained a winter outpost in the Florida Keys. The Todd Airport, a half a mile from the campus, housed a Link Trainer and three Piper Cubs that afforded interested students flight instruction and flight time.

"Skipper" Hill afloat on Todd's sixty-foot schooner, *Sea Hawk*

In the article, *Fly Your Own Plane Not Because It's Fast But Because It's Fun*, Skipper wrote:

Todd believes that hobbies and their development are of prime importance in an over-all educational plan. We have emphasized

The caption for this photograph that appeared in *Todd: A Community Devoted to Boys and Their Interests* reads: "The Seniors in their formal dinner clothes—picnic dinner." Orson is fourth from the left.

hobbies that can be carried on through adult life. Take sailing for an example. At least 100 Todd boys have enriched their lives (though possibly strained relations with their wives) through a lifelong devotion to this thrilling and rewarding avocation.

Flying, in a similar way, has enriched the lives of many Todd boys (and many of their parents) who developed an initial enthusiasm from flight instruction taken here.... My few short years as a pilot have turned me into an evangelist regarding personal flight..."

In addition to a cornucopia of out-of-the-classroom opportunities, rigorous academic standards prevailed at Todd: "In the land of youth and freedom, /Far from city's dust and noise, /Where the air is full of sunlight. /And the paths are filled with boys," quoting Orson in the Todd 1932-33 catalog.

In October 1938, *The New Yorker* observed,

Todd is a preparatory school of considerable antiquity, now run on severely progressive lines. The present headmaster, Roger Hill, a slim, white-haired, tweed-bearing man, who looks as if he had been cast for his role by a motion-picture director, has never let the traditional preparatory-school curriculum stand in the way of creative work. All the boys spend as much time as they want in the machine shop, the print shop, the bookbindery, or the school theatre.

Subsequent to shuttering the Todd School, my grandparents moved to Florida where my grandfather pursued a lifelong love of the sea, and when not sailing, operated a yacht charter service in Floridian and Bahamian waters.

He was married for sixty-six years to my grandmother, who died in 1982. They were the parents of three children, Joanne, Bette, and Roger II. My mother, Joanne, was their first born.

At Skipper's memorial in November 1990, my father captured his father-in-law's essence:

We are grouped today to remember and honor a man, a force, in each of our lives that will stay until we, too, become memory. We are not here to rend our garments, cover ourselves with ashes, and sing dirges. Keening is out. I think of the memorial as a positive thing, a brief moment to give thanks and be grateful that we were privileged to be a part of Skipper's life. I salute this man who never lost his zest for living. Until the ignominious last two years of his life, he out-hustled his destiny with projects. He had no time or tolerance for getting old. He was the only man I ever knew who out-maneuvered the vicissitudes of life and lived out his days doing exactly what he wanted to do.

His interests were catholic and he attacked them with zeal.

You were one of the chosen if you were fortunate enough to have worked with him. For those who did, he bequeathed the greatest gift one man can bestow upon another, the capacity to make you feel important in a world that often doesn't. Once embarked on one of his projects with him, he had the great wisdom to appreciate your efforts. To feel important is truly important; the gift of conveying that feeling, precious. Skipper had it.

In an interview for a Welles documentary, when asked to describe his father-in-law and the Todd School, my father remarked:

Todd was an extraordinary place and moment in time, a twenty-four hour a day utopia. Pleasure was blended with responsibility. Skipper tried to put a mature, interesting, and exciting face on whatever ventures a child pursued. His enthusiasm for theatre, movies, the sound stage, sailing, flying, or farming, to mention but a few, created this special place. The secret of life at Todd was for a student to become actively engaged in myriad facets of life in and outside the classroom, and, in the process, begin to discover and develop his talents and interests, free, in large part, of adult dictates, but rich in adult collaboration and counsel.

My father, three years Orson's junior, plays a cameo role in this book and in Orson's life. However, he played a significant part in my grandfather's life. Reflecting on my father, Orson opined to Welles biographer Barbara Leaming, "he's the one who gave up the world career to be near Roger," despite Welles's invitation to join him in the theatre. In 1936, after directing *Voodoo Macbeth*, set on an imaginary Caribbean island, with an all-African-American cast, under the aegis of the Federal Theatre Project, twenty-one-year-old Orson sent Skipper a telegram requesting my father contribute to his theatre company:

NEW YORK, NY 2:48 PM JULY-9-36
ROGER HILL—TODD SCHOOL

Government giving me theater of my own for season. Adelphi, beautiful plant near Times Square. This gives me a little gravy to hand out. I could particularly use Hascy. If this means being on relief, then so am I and my skeleton staff of principals in process of formation. Salary is $28.38 a week, but every week. Hascy would be very valuable indeed,

A contact sheet of Orson preparing a few of his many faces.

besides giving him work, a living, and connections. All my love and Virginia's [Orson's first wife]. Orson

Instead of heading east, my father enrolled at the Art Institute of Chicago.

Like Orson, my father's creativity knew no bounds. He could do anything with his head and hands: paint, sculpt, write, act, direct, build anything. Like Candide, he spent a considerable amount of time on life's small stage tending his garden wisely and devotedly.

From the time he graduated from Todd until his final curtain call, Orson affected as many public personas as he attached counterfeit noses on stage and screen. Like T.S. Eliot's refrain in "The Love Song of J. Alfred Prufrock," Orson spent a lifetime preparing many faces "to prepare to meet the faces" he encountered. Orson's authentic face was reserved for a very few, and my grandfather and grandmother were among that select group. In Skipper's presence,

Orson never had a need or desire to affect a fabricated "ORSON WELLES" persona. He was simply Skipper's devoted foster son.

During the last three years of Orson's life, my grandfather tape-recorded a number of his frequent telephone conversations with Orson to help in writing a second edition of his memoir, *One Man's Time and Chance*, and to assist Orson's penning of his life story. Unfortunately, Orson and my grandfather died before either had the opportunity to complete their respective literary projects.

Before he died, in 1990, my grandfather gave me those tapes and copies of his correspondence with Welles. After listening and reading, I was convinced that they, along with material from *Time and Chance*, could be woven into an absorbing narrative.

As an homage to Orson's and Skipper's love of the theatre, I've presented their unique friendship in the form of a play. The conversations and correspondence are authentic; like the title of Orson's never-completed Latin American "Good Neighbor Policy" film, *It's All True*. I wouldn't presume to alter the sentiments of either of the principals, but I did tighten and, on occasion, rearrange their exchanges.

The only slight flight of fancy comes at the end. The final scene is based on a telephone conversation I had with my grandfather the day after Orson's death. He described turning on his radio and hearing the doleful news that his foster son had died. Not surprisingly, Orson's death deflated my perpetually plucky and buoyant grandfather. He listened to my expressions of condolence, but no matter what I said, my words were cold comfort. Before ending our call, reflecting on the loss of his cherished friend, he drew upon one of their favorite authors, Shakespeare, "After life's fitful fever he sleeps well."

Orson was recognized by multitudes around the world, and his celebrity hasn't diminished since his death in 1985. His public persona is widely known, admired, and debated, but very few knew the private Orson Welles. That fascinating and uncommonly warm persona is radiantly revealed in every scene.

ACT ONE
PROLOGUE
LET'S PUT ON SOME PLAYS

The set consists of two libraries, one in Los Angeles, California, in the home of Orson Welles, the other, in Rockford, Illinois, in the condominium of Roger Hill. Between the two is a slightly elevated "memory diorama." Welles', the larger of the two, is stage right. In front of floor to ceiling bookcases is a large oak dining room table that serves as a desk containing an IBM electric typewriter, a large Tiffany lamp, both half buried in a mountain of script drafts, correspondence, film reels, cans, and VHS cassettes. Stage left, Hill's library consists of a couch in front of built-in bookshelves. To the right of the couch are two five-foot wooden file cabinets. Abutting the cabinets is a small roll-top desk with a Royal portable typewriter and several accordion files spread wide, all illuminated by a brass floor lamp. Between the two, center downstage, is a platform behind a translucent scrim.

Orson, behind scrim, clad in a black suit, sitting in an upholstered chair, a cigar in his right hand, speaking into a microphone, introduces Roger Hill at the Directors Guild in Los Angeles, November 1978.

ORSON: Roger Hill was a teacher in a boarding school where I was sent because of my delinquencies. I was threatened with Todd because my brother had gone there. It was then called Todd Seminary for Boys. You can imagine what it was like. It was run by Roger's father who was a God-fearing deep-water sailor and preacher who had broken the capstan bar and I don't know what else and was an extraordinary figure. Roger, known as Skipper, worked in his father's school teaching gym when I came to Todd. I tried to find a way to capture the attention of this man who fascinates me tonight as much as he did the first day I laid eyes on him. I decided that the best way was dramatics: Let's put on some plays.

Having gone to all that trouble to get his attention in the theatre, I became stuck in it. I had to learn every bit of Shakespeare because he knew it and I had to learn the entire *Bible* because he knew it.

After I left Todd, we did a series of Shakespeare textbooks, which are still in wide use. We wrote a play together and went to New York and almost sold it. He has been seen back-stage working thunder machines in any number of bravura productions of mine. He has never ceased to be my idea of who I would like to be. If I know anything at all, he taught it to me.

Roger Hill, Orson Welles, and Peter Bogdanovich, at a tribute to Orson, Working with Welles, November 1978, sponsored by the American Film Institute at the Directors Guild in Hollywood.

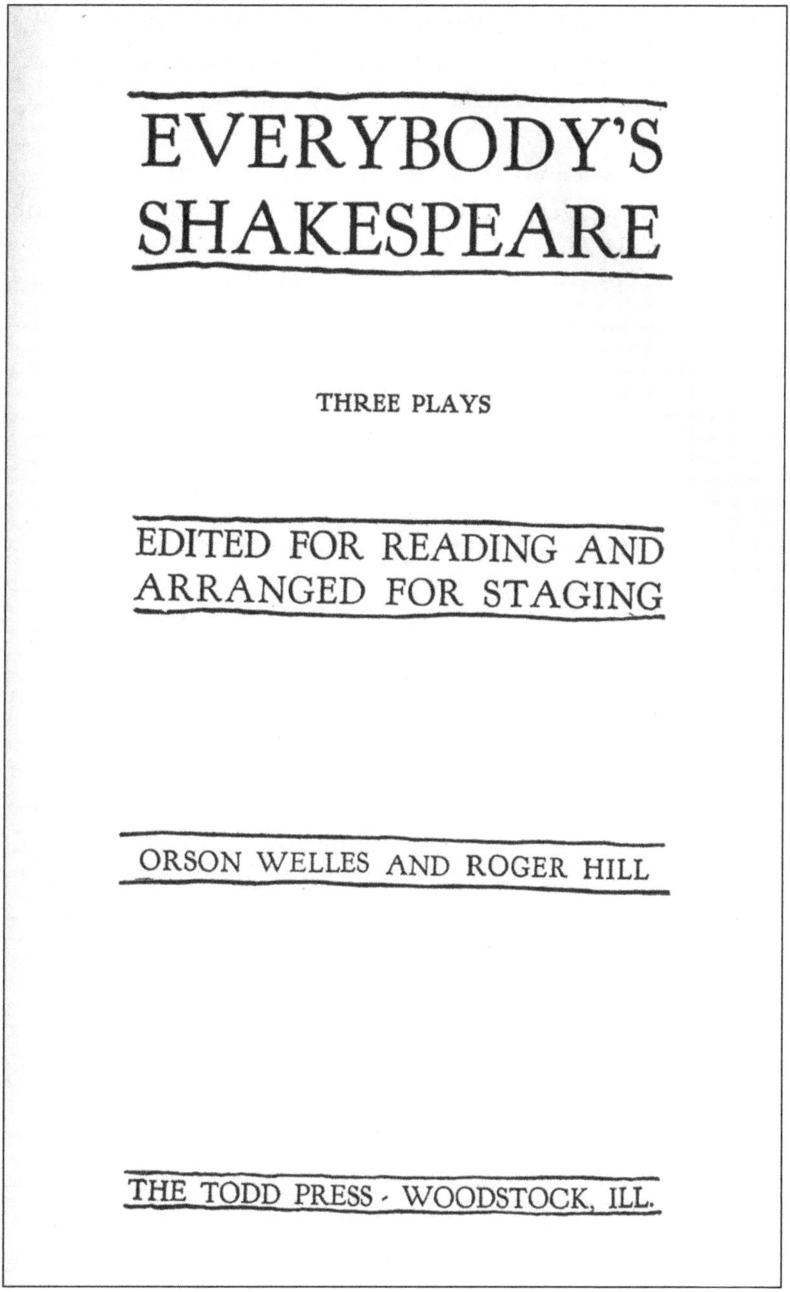

EVERYBODY'S SHAKESPEARE

THREE PLAYS

EDITED FOR READING AND ARRANGED FOR STAGING

ORSON WELLES AND ROGER HILL

THE TODD PRESS · WOODSTOCK, ILL.

Title page of the first edition of *Everybody's Shakespeare* by Orson Welles and Roger Hill, illustrations by Orson Welles, 1934.

[Lights dim.]

Ninety-year-old retired headmaster of the Todd School for Boys, Roger Hill, who, in Orson's phrase, resembles a sprightly and depraved Buffalo Bill, seated on a couch in his library, addresses the audience.

ROGER: Twice Orson introduced me with these overly exaggerated words. The first time was in November 1978 when I participated, along with Kenneth Tynan, Norman Lloyd, Dan O'Herlihy, John Berry, and Peter Bogdanovich in a tribute to Orson, *Working with Welles*, sponsored by the American Film Institute at the Directors Guild in Hollywood. The second was a November seven years later in the same Directors Guild auditorium on the occasion of Orson's memorial. Orson opened his own memorial, or, rather his voice, from a tape recording of a speech he had given at the Hollywood Foreign Press Association several years before. His subject was the movies. "The director is simply the audience," he intoned in that extraordinary voice that had changed little since our first encounter nearly sixty years ago. "So the terrible burden of the director is to take the place of that yawning vacuum, to be the audience, and to select which movement shall be a disaster and which a gala night. His job is to preside over accidents, and that's an important one." And, he ended poignantly by confessing, "I would have been much better off if, after I had made my first picture, I had gone back to the theatre from which I came. Film is the most expensive mistress that anyone could have, and I've been trying to support her ever since. It's a love you never cure yourself of." After a moment of awkward silence, the overflow audience of five hundred people broke into animated applause. At the conclusion of the applause and a brief welcome from Peter Bogdanovich, Orson's seven-year-old introduction of me was replayed to this somber gathering.

Three years before, my wife of sixty-six years, Hortense, died at 87. Orson eulogized, "Of everyone I've known, she was the most truly passionate. Yes, passionate in every good meaning of a word I choose with care. Other great and good souls may be described as warm or warm-hearted. That's too tepid sounding for Hortense. Warm is a word for comfort and consolation. The word for her was Heat. Fire. The very element itself. She has gone away and left a black hole in our universe. And yet to mourn is to remember. That shining, vivid, marvelously living presence is back with us again and our hearts are stabbed with happiness. For just to think of her can never be anything but an occasion for joy."

Orson's words of tribute perfectly defined their author, as well. For years, I encouraged Orson to capture and share "that shining, vivid, marvelously living presence" in a memoir. Each time I broached the subject, he adroitly and charmingly dodged. When I urged him to keep a journal with the thought of publication, he responded, "When I grow too old to make movies, then I'll think of picking up a pen and gazing into a mirror. This business of writing one's memoir is an act of extreme ego and pretension. Even the very word 'memoir' seems to me terribly pompous."

He never grew too old to make movies. However, several years before he died, a number of publishers joined me in urging him to write his memoir. His resistance to writing "my book," as he began to call it, began to wane. "Being in show business, I'm well-endowed with a healthy ego," he confessed, "or else I wouldn't stand up in front of the public for six decades and have the presumption to ask my audience to be quiet. But, to write a book about

myself and to proclaim to the world, 'Hey, I'm
Orson Welles and what I have to say is worth
attending,' would be an embarrassment. I don't
like looking into the mirror. I far prefer looking
through a lens, and focusing outward rather than
inward." I continued to hector and publishers
continued to cajole and offer ever more tempting
advances. The offers, he confessed, were flattering
and the money tempting. But the energy it would
take to write, he insisted, would take time from
his unflagging efforts to complete *The Other Side
of the Wind, The Dreamers, The Big Brass Ring,*
and *The Magic Show,* and to begin filming *The
Cradle Will Rock* and *Lear.*

Finally, in 1982, Orson wrote a personal essay in
the December '82/January '83 issue of *Paris Vogue.*
He found this brief glimpse into the mirror not the
discomforting exercise he had imagined. To the
contrary, it ignited a desire to begin a book, not so
much a chronology of his life, but a collection of
impressions of his world. He knew that I had
begun taping our frequent telephone conversations
to assist in revising and expanding my family
chronicle, *One Man's Time and Chance.* He asked
that I save these tapes for the day he would begin
to write his autobiographic sketchbook. Time ran
out before he could begin extricating from the
tapes. Fortunately, however, "That shining, vivid,
marvelously living presence is back with us again,"
and I hope throughout the performance your
heart will be stabbed with happiness.

As an actor, his characters ranged from the
vainglorious Charles Foster Kane to the corrupt
Hank Quinlan, from an inspirational Abraham
Lincoln to a conspiring John D. Rockefeller. As a
journalist and radio commentator, his subjects

ranged from championing Franklin Delano Roosevelt's New Deal to examining atomic testing in the Pacific. One role he never played was himself—until now.

[Lights dim.]

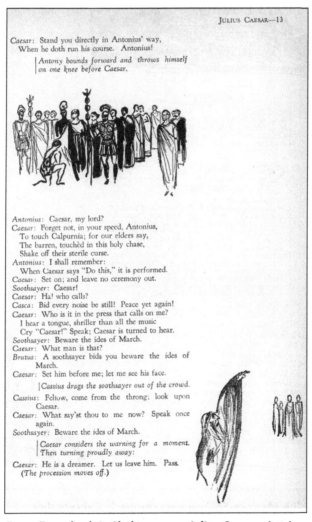

From *Everybody's Shakespeare, Julius Caesar,* Act I, Scene I

MACBETH

Stage business set in this manner (behind vertical lines) is in addition to that recorded phonographically on Mercury Text Records. On these records the cast acts the entire play and a narrator adds the descriptive matter enclosed in parentheses.

ACT I
SCENE I

SCOTLAND
A desert place

Source of the plot:
Shakespeare used Holinshed's *Chronicle of England and Scotland* as the basis for many of his plays. In the case of *Macbeth* he used it as the sole basis. Just as in the case of *Julius Caesar* and North's *Plutarch* the parallelism is continuous, the play being simply a versification and dramatization of the source material. It is completely fascinating to have this intimate view into Shakespeare's very study, in effect to look over his shoulder as he pens his thunderous lines. Set in small type before each of the following scenes are excerpts from the Holinshed material which lay in front of the dramatist as he worked.

(*Enter three Witches.*)
First Witch: When shall we three meet again? In thunder, lightning, or in rain?
Second Witch: When the hurlyburly's done,
When the battle's lost, and won.
Third Witch: That will be ere the set of sun.
First Witch: Where the place?
Second Witch: Upon the heath.
Third Witch: There to meet with Macbeth.
First Witch: I come, Graymalkin.
Second Witch: Paddock calls:
First Witch: Anon!
Third Witch: Fair is foul,
Second Witch: And foul is fair.
All: Hover through the fog and filthy air.
| *They exit.*

From *The Mercury Shakespeare* (formerly *Everybody's Shakespeare*), *Macbeth*, Act I, Scene I

ACT ONE
SCENE ONE

NOVEMBER 25, 1982
STEP BACK JOHN BARRYMORE, GORDON CRAIG,
AND JOHN CLAYTON, YOUR DAY HAS PASSED

At the rise of the curtain, Orson is sitting upstage on a couch reading a book in his Las Vegas home he shares with his wife, Paola Mori, and their daughter Beatrice. He stops reading, places the book on a coffee table in front of him that is chock-a-block with an amalgam of books, newspapers and a telephone. He picks up the phone and dials. Hill is sitting at his desk in a captain's chair typing on a Royal typewriter. The telephone rings and Roger picks up the receiver.

Welles-Hill libraries, Thanksgiving Day.

ROGER: Hello.

ORSON: Roger, Happy Thanksgiving. How are you?

ROGER: I'm all right. I was listening to the tape I made of our recent call.

ORSON: I didn't know that you made a tape of that call, but then—

ROGER: I tape everybody.

ORSON: You've become a CIA man.

ROGER: That's right.

ORSON: When I last called, you pretended that you couldn't get the recorder to work. You stuttered, "It's not recording, oh, never mind. We'll talk without recording."

ROGER: You're a better liar than I am. No, actually—

ORSON: No, you're a terrible liar. It isn't as though you don't try.

ROGER: No. I told you, "Look, I'm going to start taping our conversations to help gather material to update the chapter on you in my revised memoir and help you write your memoir."

ORSON: And then you said, "I can't get it to work."

ROGER: No, that was an earlier conversation. You're mixed up. Are you sober?

ORSON: I haven't had a drink in years.

ROGER: Well, are you any healthier?

ORSON: No. I just don't drink.

ROGER: You don't smoke either, except for awful cigars once in a while.

ORSON: Except those awful cigars. Have you eaten your turkey dinner?

ROGER: Yes, and wonderfully cooked by Hascy.

ORSON: Paola is cooking a duck and the whole house smells good.

ROGER: And what is Beatrice doing these days?

ORSON: Beatrice is in love and in love with life. I wish she would take a serious turn at acting. She says she's interested, but I don't know how serious she is.

To Roper e Hortense with our fondest love always —

Orson

Photograph of Paola Mori, Orson's third wife, and their child, Beatrice, sent from Orson to Roger and Hortense Hill, 1956.

ROGER: She needs experience that she currently lacks.

ORSON: She could have experience, but so far, she chooses not to compete and work for little money.

ROGER: Oh, she'll find her way either in acting or something. You didn't make a great salary in Ireland.

ORSON: But I was playing star parts in a capital city of
           Europe at sixteen.

ROGER: But you didn't just step off a boat and land on the
           Dublin stage. You traveled to Ireland to paint and
           escape Harvard.

ORSON: True, and I fell in love with Ireland the moment I
           stepped ashore on the Aran Islands. I never painted
           as much as I did in Ireland.

ROGER: You kept telling us you were going to send us some
           of your paintings, but you traded them for food
           and lodging as you wandered the country on your
           bicycle, Ulysses, and later on your donkey cart.
           Thank God you didn't deal away your journal
           chronicling your two-week barge trip down the
           Shannon that ends with the ribald saga of a young
           couple on the Battery in the citadel city of
           Athlone.

SCRIM: *Sixteen-year-old Orson, sitting on a donkey-cart, writing in
his journal.*

The hill of which I have spoken is called the Battery and is crossed
by a stone-breasted gully impregnable from vulgar gaze. There I came
upon three little boys, their bellies flat upon the grass, peeping
furtively over the brink. I tiptoed up behind them to see what the
object of their attention was and was amused to discover two young
persons of the opposite sex reclining in the trench and making violent
and enthusiastic love. But what delighted both performers and audience
most was the presence of a matronly lady—fat in a respectable kind of
way—and obviously the chaperone of the party—snoring lustily
alongside the delighted lovers!

Rather than disturb so happy a scene, I descended the hill on the
side farthest from Romeo and his dark-eyed Juliet. This brought

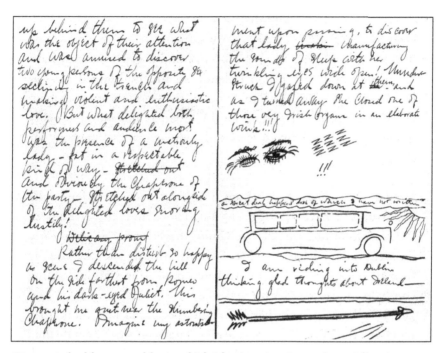

"A great deal happened here which I have not written. I am riding into Dublin thinking glad thoughts about Ireland."

me quite near the slumbering chaperone. Imagine my astonishment upon passing, to discover that lady manufacturing the sounds of sleep with her twinkling eyes wide open! Dumbstruck, I gazed down at them and, as I turned away, one of those very Irish organs closed in an elaborate wink!!!!

[Lights dim.]

ORSON: Yes, I wrote that while riding on my donkey-cart from Galway to Dublin.

ROGER: And into the bright dawn of your stage career at the Gate Theatre.

[Center downstage behind a translucent scrim, Orson sits alone in the back row of the Gate Theatre writing a letter.]

Dear Skipper,

A donkey cart, a bicycle, a port-barge and a gypsy caravan have taken me round and round Ireland and finally dumped me—as Dr. must by this time have told you, in the Gate Theatre—Dublin. Here I shall probably remain until Christmas and more probably spring—playing, painting scenery and signs, and writing publicity for the press...

Need I tell you how happy I am in this arrangement? Here is the opportunity I have been praying for. The Gate is just organized. We are a kind of Irish Theatre Guild, that is to say an art theatre on a commercial basis.... Mr. Hilton Edwards and the equally formal Micheál mac Liammóir, had a producing staff and acting company of really exceptional people—neither mellowed and jaded "old-timers" and hams, nor inexperienced beginners, they represent the best of that vast army—larger on these islands than cross-Atlantic, which the talkies have reduced (them) to job hunting...

A part of the present company was rallied together from cross-channel, native Irish, and British colonial sources—and the Gate Theatre opened with *Peer Gynt* in the late spring. I really didn't think such a company existed—where people were serious minded, highly intelligent, and well-educated, and combined these virtues with the more cardinal sense of humor—wholesomeness—and rationality...

There are fifteen professionals in the company besides the technical staff, the directors, dancers, and musicians. Everybody works "for the joy of working, and each in his separate sphere." The phrase "nobody works for money" being particularly applicable—salaries are of chorus girls' dimensions and are all of the same amount regardless of one's position...

I went to the Gate on my second evening in Dublin simply for entertainment's sweet sake. The play was new and native. The acting was good in spite of it and I was delighted to see my old friend Cathal O'Callaigh, whom I had known in the North, doing quite well in one of the smaller roles. I waited at the stage door and, in the course of time we met, visited, and arranged a later meeting at the theatre. It was then that I met Hilton, our dynamic, hot-tempered and golden-hearted Lord of Lords. There was much talk and finally an application for a job. He was gracious and candid. He would be delighted, he said, but the budget would not permit another member. He could find me a small part in *Jew Süss*, just going into rehearsal, but I would have to work on amateur's wages—which are but a gesture. If I care to stick it out, and if we got along, bigger parts might come and he might even persuade the committee to pay me an extra Guinea—I accepted.

There are two big parts in *Jew Süss*. One is the George Arliss title role and the other is the half Emil Jannings, half Douglas Fairbanks contrast to the Jew, Karl Alexander, and the Duke. I read the play, decided I had no chance as Süss, and though I scarcely dared dream of getting it, learned Karl Alexander. My first audition was a bitter failure. I read a scene and being terribly nervous and anxious to impress, I performed a kind of J Worthington Ham bit with all the tricks and resonance I could conjure up. The real climax to the whole thing is that Charles Margood—actor—press agent and assistant scene painter has left and I am hired in his place to fill the various departments in which he functioned! Step back John Barrymore, Gordon Craig, and John Clayton, your day has passed. A new glory glows in the East. I am a professional!!!

[Lights dim.]

Portrait Orson sent to Roger and Hortense Hill from Dublin, Ireland, 1931.

ROGER: But, we were talking about Beatrice. Maybe acting isn't what she really wants to pursue.

ORSON: She's not sure what she wants to do. She has the chance to go to New York and move around in the great world. I hope she takes it. She's got everything on the ball, and I tell her so, but she doesn't seem to believe it.

ROGER: She has to have other people tell her she's talented, because it doesn't matter what her father or mother say. It takes time for most of us, an awful lot of time, to finally figure out what we want to do. That was certainly true for me.

ORSON: You've figured it out? I haven't figured it out yet.

ROGER: [Roger laughs] Yes you have.

ORSON: No I haven't.

ROGER: You seemed to know very early on what you wanted to do.

ORSON: I did not. All the things I wanted to do I never did.

ROGER: What did you want to do?

ORSON: Almost everything else. Beatrice is a very attractive young girl that people take a shine to, and I've told her that she would do well to enter a cosmopolitan and competitive atmosphere for a bit, even, if later, she decides she wants to spend the rest of her life in a small town smelling the flowers.

ROGER: What's new with you?

ORSON: Nothing is new with me.

ROGER: Honestly? Then why don't you come for a visit?

ORSON: I'd like that sooner than later. But for the next few months, I'm happily burdened with projects in California and Europe.

ROGER: Is the cost of living cheaper in Europe?

ORSON: California is cheaper than any European country I know.

ROGER: That just doesn't make sense with the English pound—

ORSON: The pound is down, but inflation is tremendous. Housing in every European country, not just England, is so much more expensive than in America, renting or buying, anything to do with a roof over your head. If you bring dollars to Europe, everything's a bargain because of the exchange.

ROGER: Paola likes England, doesn't she?

ORSON: She loves England and so does Beatrice.

ROGER: Do they both enjoy living in the United States?

ORSON: They do. Paola thinks England is better, but she likes it here. When you've lived in a number of countries, you always like the country you're not in.

ROGER: I can relate. The same is true when you've lived in various areas of this country. [Gentle laughter] There is much I miss about Southern Florida, the ocean, sailing, and weather. But, when I begin to miss that paradise, I remind myself of the hurricane season, the steamy, terrarium-like summers, and the Biblical infestation of toads that were brought from South America to keep the mosquito population at bay.

ORSON: That reminds me, I was in Alsace, near Strasbourg, making a picture a while back. It's the country where the stork is a national symbol for good fortune and prosperity. Not many years ago, there was a stork on every fence in the countryside, which provided a dramatic vista. Now, the stork population is declining precipitously due to the paving over and drying up of swamps. That reduced the number of frogs, which is a staple of the stork's diet. There go the storks.

ROGER: Our toads are not food for anything, they're just pests. They have a poison sac and if a dog bites one, it's likely to become paralyzed.

ORSON: These toads are really poisonous? I always thought it was a childish superstition.

ROGER: Or a Shakespearean one. *"Sweet are the uses of adversity, /which, like a toad, ugly and venomous, /Wears yet a precious jewel in his head; /And this our life, exempt from public haunt, /Finds tongues in trees, books in the running brooks, /Sermons in stones, and good in everything."*

ORSON: Dogs are a problem in our peripatetic household. A six-month quarantine was required to take them out of England. We've always had dogs as you know. We had one dog we brought from Spain to England. They put it in quarantine, and while he was in solitary confinement, the poor dog died of a broken heart.

ROGER: How about all those felines that you picked up all over Spain? Is your Las Vegas home a sanctuary for a clutch of cats?

ORSON: Oh, yes. Everywhere.

ROGER: Is your place in Los Angeles a menagerie?

ORSON: Kiki, my sweet serpent-toothed black poodle, and I are inseparable. She goes with me everywhere, the rest stay in Las Vegas. I was reluctant to buy a home in California because the property tax is scary. You wake up one morning to discover that your house is worth five times more than when you bought it a few years earlier. California pays for everything out of property taxes, which I think is unfair. Of course, it's old people and retired people who suffer the most.

ROGER: Shortly before Horty died, there was talk in Illinois of increasing the sales tax on food.

ORSON: Which is also undemocratic. The poor person pays as much as the rich one.

ROGER: It's regressive. In a moment of pique, after learning of the proposed increase, Horty howled, "To show our displeasure, we should stop eating." [Orson roars]. You couldn't always expect logic from Hortense, but always passion.

ORSON: What's better than passion? I, too, have an impassioned wife. She puts Hortense to shame. Paola becomes excited and worries if nothing is going wrong because it hasn't started yet. But she's wonderful when things are very bad. She's just crazy as hell about small things.

Hortense and Roger Hill, 1979

ROGER: You've been spending quite a bit of time in
          California and cutting back on work in Europe.

ORSON: Yes, there's a good deal of work keeping me busy in
          Hollywood. I've opted to work less in Europe
          because plane travel flattens me. My theory is that
          it's much easier flying on the prop planes. I believe
          there is a mystery to it besides the difference in
          time.

ROGER: It may be the altitude.

ORSON: It may be the pressure and altitude. I have noticed that when you make a long trip, the fatigue seems to come in the last forty minutes, no matter how long or short the trip when you're losing altitude. I bet someday they'll find it has something to do with that. Before jets, prop planes offered Pullman arrangements, with upper and lower berths. It was wonderful. There's something deflating in today's jet age that requires you to sit up all night in a glorified bus.

ROGER: How true. Horty and I took a month-long trip around the world several years ago. On each leg, I had to get up and walk around because there was much too much sitting, especially the flight from Japan to Hawaii. We were with SANE, a peace group, commemorating the twenty-fifth anniversary of the Hiroshima bombing. In Hiroshima, we stayed in the home of Japanese survivors, thanks to a good friend, Barbara Reynolds, who lived in Hiroshima for fifteen years after the war promoting world peace. She and her former husband, Earle, sailed their yacht, the *Phoenix*, into South Pacific waters that were declared off limits during the 1958 Eniwetok Atoll nuclear bomb tests. Earle's arrest and subsequent trial brought them world-wide attention.

ORSON: I admire their courage.

ROGER: Barbara and Earle were Quakers, and before heading for Japan, they stopped at Todd and left their son with us. He was enrolled for a year before joining his parents in Hiroshima. When the Reynolds arrived on campus, neither had been near the sea. After seeing movies of the Todd schooners, Earle became excited and told us that as a child he read Joshua Slocum's book, *Sailing Alone Around the*

World. It whetted Earle's interest in sailing and he hoped to one day sail around the world. He had a little money, but he had heard that there were several idle shipyards in Hiroshima. He asked me, were he to buy a boat, what would I recommend. I remember suggesting he consider a double-ender for its seaworthiness and an outboard rudder. I suggested a ketch rig or possibly a staysail schooner. He eventually bought a yacht in Japan, and four years later, he and his family sailed from Hiroshima on the ketch, *Phoenix.* They circled the globe and wrote a book, *All in the Same Boat.* He wrote a second book entitled *The Forbidden Voyage,* an account of his arrest and trial.

ORSON: That's a remarkable tale, the stuff of a great screenplay.

ROGER: Reynolds is quoted in the book I'm working on, based on the anti-war film we produced at Todd, *Rip Van Winkle Renascent.* Hascy and I co-wrote it and Hascy directed the Todd production. In addition to the script, I'm including an introduction that touches on Bob Wilson, my cousin, and his activities at Los Alamos, and our work at Todd with the American Friends Service Committee.

ORSON: I look forward to reading your tome.

ROGER: When it's further along, I'll send you a draft.

ORSON: I will hold you to that promise. My God, Roger, what a joy to talk to you.

ROGER: The joy is mine. Thanks for calling.

ORSON: I'll call again soon. Bye.

[Lights dim.]

Rip Van Winkle Renascent screenplay cover illustrated by my father.

ACT ONE
SCENE TWO

FEBRUARY 22, 1983
WHAT DIDN'T I DO ON THE RADIO?

At the rise of the curtain, Orson is sitting behind the desk in an expansive white high-backed chair in the Los Angeles home that he shared with Oja Kodar, his muse and collaborator for the last twenty-four years of his life. (All of Orson's subsequent scenes take place in his Los Angeles residence.) He stops pecking at his typewriter, picks up the phone and dials. Roger is sitting at his desk in a captain's chair reading. The telephone rings and Roger picks up the receiver.

ROGER: Hello.

ORSON: Roger?

ROGER: So, how are you?

ORSON: I'm fine, and you?

ROGER: Oh [Extended pause], I'm swell.

ORSON: C'mon. You sound tentative. What's up?

ROGER: I'm worried about my goddamned brain. All of a sudden my body and brain are becoming dilapidated. I have vivid recall of my youth, and the distant past. I can quote the *Bible*, Shakespeare, and a great deal of poetry I learned as a child. But, I can't recall with such clarity what happened last week, or last month.

ORSON: You know damn well the early stuff is better than the late stuff. Wouldn't it be awful if it were the other way around? What the hell is there to remember about last month? The great stuff is still with us. Cling to those treasured thoughts. [Laughter]

ROGER: I was surprised the other day when my grand-daughter asked me about the Sermon on the Mount, "Blessed are the poor in spirit: for theirs is the kingdom of heaven. Blessed are they that mourn: for they shall be comforted. Blessed are the meek: for they shall inherit the earth. Blessed are they which do hunger and thirst after righteousness: for they shall be filled. Blessed are the merciful: for they shall obtain mercy. Blessed are the pure in heart: for they shall see God. Blessed are the peacemakers: for they shall be called the children of God. Blessed are they which are persecuted for righteousness' sake: for theirs is the kingdom of heaven." I was able to recite the entire Sermon on the Mount.

ORSON: The Russian actor, Akim Tamiroff and his wife Tamara Shayne were great friends of mine. His wife was an azure-eyed beauty in her youth, and she still was quite beautiful when I knew her. They had been together for more than thirty years when, one afternoon, she was sitting with two or three other women playing bridge and Akim was in the adjoining bedroom resting. She began in a very animated fashion telling her friends about, "How he can be so utterly foolish at times." At which point, one of her guests inquired, "Whom are you talking about?" She said, "Ah, ah, who am I talking about, you know who I'm talking about, ah, ah, wait a minute, the one I sleep with!" [Laughter] She dried up on her husband's name.

ROGER: You're kidding.

ORSON: I have dried up on the names I know best.

ROGER: Oh, you're unbelievable. You can remember
             absolutely everything that ever happened.

ORSON: No, I have your trouble too. I have so much
             business to discuss all the time—taxes, visas,
             movies that are going to be made, not made, but
             have tremendous contractual contingencies, and
             I'm reminded of things that I said and things
             that I don't remember saying. I just bluff my way
             through. I can remember everything that happened
             at Todd, but I just can't remember everything that
             happened on the corner of Hollywood and Vine;
             and I don't want to, either. [Laughter] Is that your
             worst worry?

ROGER: Sure.

ORSON: Well, that's why you should be spending some time
             with me because I don't care what happened last
             week either. I want to tap the sources of your real
             wisdom.

ROGER: [Laughing] That's another thing. I'm always afraid
             people will really find me out. I'm a Goddamn
             bluffer and the only talent I ever had was that
             people, many of whom were brighter than I, liked
             me.

ORSON: Did it ever occur to you why these people like you?

ROGER: No. It's a mystery.

ORSON: Well, let me tell you why. It's because you're
             brighter than you think you are.

ROGER: I am not. I've always leaned on you. I've been thinking about that lately.

ORSON: You haven't leaned on me. Never. I was the one who leaned on you from our first encounter until this very moment. You inspired people, not leaned on them. You dare to speak about that? You don't know what you've been. If there's anybody who's half worth anything in your life, you have had made them worth more. You are the opposite of parasitic: you're a giver, not a taker. But you formed, at a very early age, probably in your teens, the idea that the cute way to get around in the world was to underplay yourself, and to say that you're a fake and all that kind of thing, and that your self-criticism would enchant people. I'm sorry to say that I imitated that. And it's cost me a great deal of money through the years, because when I say something like that with overwhelming self-criticism, everybody believes me. [Laughter] I exaggerate. I'm extravagant in my negative self-appraisal. I have a much better opinion of myself. But I do this thing that in the motion picture industry—you should excuse the expression—is called "kicking the shit under the rug." You know how the cowboy used to kick his boots down on the ground?

ROGER: Yes.

ORSON: "Kicking the shit under the rug." I picked it up from you and it's the only damn bad thing you did for me, because in this world people take you for the value that you give yourself. You've always been convinced that it's charming and the greatest goddamned trick in the world, depending on how you want to explain it, selling yourself short. And you have finally convinced yourself that it's true and here you are babbling away telling me that you've leaned on people, when you've lit the lamp in so many places that it can't be numbered. So, when can I expect a visit?

ROGER: I'm going to get rid of some things and then come out to see you. Oh, if I could only get rid of this damn noise. Talk about troubles. The noise of my heartbeat is in my ears and goes "ptut, ptut, ptut."

ORSON: They can't stop it?

ROGER: They can't stop it. I'll say this, at least it tells me all the time how regular or irregular my damn heartbeat is.

ORSON: Have you asked the doctors if they can stop it?

ROGER: No, I haven't.

ORSON: Well, you should. No one should be hearing "ptut, ptut, ptut" all the time. I don't think you should be hearing your heartbeat day and night. You'll end up like the fellow in the last paragraph of Edgar Allen Poe's "The Tell-Tale Heart," you'll confess to everything! The protagonist dispatches the old man, cuts him into pieces, and buries him under the floor, but he can't escape the sound of the old man's beating heart. It would be a great one-man, one-act play. At the end he suddenly yells, "Yes, yes, tear it up, he's there." That was the telltale part. I did it on the radio once. What didn't I do on the radio?

ROGER: That's right, come to think of it.

ORSON: I never did "The Cask of Amontillado."

ROGER: You didn't brick up Fortunado?

ORSON: No, but I put him in a script once. A movie that
             was to be made by three directors, and I was
             supposed to be one of them. Each of us was going
             to do a horror story. I wrote mine and then they
             never got the money. I combined "The Cask of
             Amontillado" with "Ligeia." How the hell I did it I
             can't remember, but I did. The poem, "The
             Conqueror Worm," the last words of "Ligeia,"
             become more poignant with every passing year:
             "Lo 'tis a gala night /Within the lonesome latter
             years! /An angel throng, bewinged, bedight /In
             veils, and drowned in tears, /Sit in a theatre, to
             see /A play of hopes and fears. /While the orchestra
             breathes fitfully /The music of the spheres" and
             ends "The curtain, a funeral pall, /Comes down
             with the rush of a storm, /And the angels, all pallid
             and wan, /Uprising, unveiling, affirm /That the
             play is the tragedy, 'Man,' /And its hero the
             Conqueror Worm." Do you remember "The
             Masque of the Red Death"? It's a Poe classic.

ROGER: Not too well.

ORSON: Poe begins by describing a devastating epidemic,
             the "Red Death." To flee the pandemic, Prince
             Prospero and a thousand noblemen hole up in an
             abbey. The plague swirls beyond the walls of the
             abbey and kills the disenfranchised who are forced
             to live outside the walls. A half year into their
             secure existence, the prince entertains friends at a
             masked ball. At the stroke of twelve midnight, a
             spectral figure, the Red Death, appears, and kills
             all the revelers. How did Poe conclude? Oh, yes,
             "And Darkness and Decay and the Red Death held
             illimitable dominion over all." But "The Tell-Tale
             Heart" would be a great sketch for somebody to do

because it's a monologue and it's well written. It's not a word too long, and nobody else speaks. I don't know why I never made it as a short in a movie because it's one of his best.

ROGER: Do you ever find yourself missing radio?

ORSON: Radio is what I love most of all. The wonderful excitement of what could happen in live radio, when everything that could go wrong did go wrong. I was making a couple of thousand a week, scampering in ambulances from studio to studio, and committing much of what I made to support the Mercury. I wouldn't want to return to those frenetic twenty-hour working day years, but I miss them because they are so irredeemably gone.

ROGER: You were the excitement! My God, I remember like it was last week, your calling me after your *War of the Worlds* broadcast, in a breathless state, over the nationwide flap your show had produced.

ORSON: What a night. After the broadcast, as I tried to get back to the St. Regis where we were living, I was blocked by an impassioned crowd of news people looking for blood, and the disappointment when they found I wasn't hemorrhaging. It wasn't long after the initial shock that whatever public panic and outrage there was vanished. But, the newspapers for days continued to feign fury.

ROGER: The newspapers considered the radio a new and real threat.

ORSON: Yes, the newspapers had been fighting radio as an advertising medium for years. Hundreds of editorials ranted about how irresponsible CBS and Welles were, insisting that I would never be offered another job in show business and how lucky I was not to be in jail. Most self-serving of all, they assured their readers that newspapers would never sink to such reckless disregard for the public's welfare. Gary Graver's just arrived, and I must reluctantly leave you.

ROGER: Bye. Talk to you soon.

ORSON: Soon.

[Lights dim.]

"Radio is what I love most of all. The wonderful excitement of what could happen in live radio, when everything that could go wrong did go wrong."

Orson, director, William Robson, and Archibald MacLeish preparing the April 11, 1937 *Columbia Workshop* radio broadcast of MacLeish's *Fall of the City.*

ACT ONE
SCENE THREE

MARCH 14, 1983
ALL LIFE IS ONE FORM OF DECEPTION
OR ANOTHER

Interior of Roger and Orson's libraries. Roger's telephone rings.

ROGER: Hello?

ORSON: Roger, how are you?

ROGER: Fine. I've been away for a few days in Chicago and I just—

ORSON: You can go to Chicago, but you can't go to Los Angeles?

ROGER: [Laughing] I'll get out to see you soon after I finish some writing chores. But, you know where I'm tempted to go now?

ORSON: Sail to Capri?

ROGER: I used to think that if I ever had any time I might want to sail in exotic waters. In my youth, Capri and Zanzibar and a hundred other romantic-sounding destinations held my imagination captive. In my ninth decade, I have absolutely no desire to do my own cruising. What intrigues me now is the opera in New York. When I was young, I used to go to the opera in Chicago with my mother and uncle, Joe Rogers, the music critic for *The*

Philadelphia Inquirer. After a long lifetime, I would like to experience an opera or two in New York.

ORSON: Anything but to see me.

ROGER: No. You know I'm going to see you, but you must appreciate my desire to attend several operas in New York.

ORSON: The new Metropolitan is terrible.

ROGER: It is?

ORSON: The old Metropolitan was much better. The seats were more comfortable and the productions much better.

ROGER: Really?

ORSON: Currently, the best opera is in San Francisco, Santa Fe, and New Orleans. All the good stuff is happening outside New York. The Met is really nothing extraordinary except as a venue to showcase a Prima Donna Absoluta, of which there are only two or three in any period. Beverly Sills retired seven years ago. She's the impresario. New York critics are always praising what's happening in San Francisco and in Philadelphia. Opera, in general, has come upon evil days. It's all in the hands of the stage directors. They're always asking me to direct operas and I always refuse because I don't think the boss of the opera ought to be the stage director. I think it ought to be the conductor and then the next bosses ought to be the leading performers. The stage directors today are doing tricky revisions of the operas and spoiling the intentions of the composer for the most part.

ROGER: It's the theatrics not the conductor that is key; a
           conductor plays a more perfunctory role.

ORSON: The director stages the opera, supervises the stage
           design, gives the actors their movements, and
           directs the opera like it was a play. There's always
           been a stage director as well as a conductor. No, I
           don't think you'll miss a thing by not going to New
           York for opera. You can travel shorter distances and
           see something much more original and better.
           When they ask me to stage an opera, they don't
           expect me to wave my arms in front of the orchestra.
           They ask me to tell singers where to stand, design
           or supervise the design of the sets and costumes,
           and have a plan for the opera. If I decided that
           it would be cute to have *La Boheme* done in a
           contemporary neo-hippie setting, I'd do it. That's
           the kind of thing that has spoiled so much opera,
           and I've steadfastly refused. You don't know how
           many offers I receive to direct in Europe and in
           America. I don't want to because I think that
           people expect me to do something different and I
           want to take all that elaborate difference out of
           opera and return to what Verdi wanted it to be, or
           Bellini or whomever, and not try to show how
           smart I am. The great opera composers knew the
           theatre as well as the great playwrights. They knew
           the effects that they wanted and that should be
           followed. That doesn't mean deadly tradition-
           bound productions. It means a basic respect for
           the material, rather than respect for yourself and
           showmanship.

ROGER: Don't the tenors get much more publicity now
           than the women?

ORSON: They always did. As Pavarotti says, "A great tenor is
           making an unnatural and impossible sound." You

see this is not true of baritones and bassos. I always remember what Caruso said to my mother. I never knew Caruso, but she told me, he said, "I always remember that the audience is entirely composed of tenors. I know that when I hit a high note, I try to make it look hard. It's easy for me, but by making it look hard the whole audience feels that I've accomplished something and I get a big hand. [Laughter] You hear those old records of his through the horn, and they make your hair stand on end, they're so great.

ROGER: That's right. My grandmother and my mother had all those Victor Red Seal records of Caruso.

ORSON: We did, too, in our house. But I never, even as a child, got to meet him. He used to be in the house a lot before I was born and when I was a baby. There's a cartoon that he made of my mother at the piano. He was a very good cartoonist, and a tremendous, tremendous singer, of course. The greatest soprano I ever heard was Claudia Muzio, and that was in our lifetime. She sang in Chicago. You can get marvelous records of hers and she makes everybody else sound like a bum. I love the opera; it's my favorite form of theatre and always has been. That's why it dumbfounds people, when I refuse to have anything to do with it. But, so much for opera.

ROGER: The other big question on my mind is taxes. How about you? I'm behind and I promise to get it in. I haven't even given my figures to my accountant who says he has to have them.

ORSON: I was given a delay because I have a poor set of invoices. I can't justify a lot of stuff and it turns out that, in the last few years, I've not been paying a lot of taxes that I needed to pay. I ran out of my old age pension. You can get too old for it. Did you know that?

ROGER: No. What the hell are you talking about?

ORSON: There is a tax arrangement where you can put aside money for retirement and then you can either pay taxes on part of this money every year or you can delay it until you get the money. Eventually, you pay taxes. But you don't pay interest during that time. It's a way to put aside money for a time when you might be making less. But I didn't pay the taxes on the pension because my accountant didn't think of it. Now I have to pay a fine of $280,000. So, don't mention taxes to me unless you want me to have a miserable night of melancholy.

ROGER: [Laughing] Oh, that's too bad.

ORSON: I've been a victim of tax situations all my life.

ROGER: All your life.

ORSON: Clever people hired to help me gave me the wrong advice. Now, as your devoted friend who adores you, I beg you to remove yourself for a time from writing *The Rise and Fall of the Roman Empire*, charging about in your convertible, and entertaining your ever-enlarging family. Pause and come spend some time with me.

ROGER: I will come out, but I must make progress on my book. You'll probably sneer at what I'm trying to do, but it's not—

ORSON: You misunderstand me. I don't sneer. I could never sneer at anything you do. But, I am concerned that

Orson and my father designed an elaborate puppet theatre, fashioned a dozen marionettes, and Orson directed a melodrama set in the J.P. Bloodshed Bank, whose president, Julius Peabody, was the play's "dastardly villain." The second half of the evening's entertainment was a lively musical revue performed by puppets resembling faculty members.

you have given yourself, as always, gigantic projects. Luckily, you've reached an age where it's no longer possible for you to lie and say it's a project by the Todd boys.

ROGER: [Laughs] "Done by the boys"—Orson and Hascy.

ORSON: "Done by the boys in their own workshop."

ROGER: I was a phony in lots of ways and I admit it.

ORSON: You're not phony. You're self-effacing, if you want to call that phony. Self-effacing is the opposite of ego. Admirable in every respect.

ROGER: Admirable except that it was untrue, as you reminded me recently, that I was self-effacing in my youth, which, I guess, makes me guilty of deception.

ORSON: All life is one form of deception or another. Your deception always was benevolent and never anything else. If you think I'm sneering at what you're doing, you're very wrong. I'm making good fun of it in an attempt to get you to simplify the job. But sneering is not the word at all. I'm sure your revision of *Time and Chance* will be absolutely fascinating, and I mean that sincerely. You've created a gigantic task coupled with a terrible sense of urgency, which the beating of wings in your ears exacerbates, no doubt.

ROGER: Yes.

ORSON: Simplify.

ROGER: The beating of wings in my ears certainly adds a sense of urgency. Writing is great therapy.

ORSON: Everybody is his or her own doctor. Some very good doctors say that everybody is essentially their own doctor, and that's true. I just don't want you to drown in an undertow of your literary exertions. I'd like you to be an honest peacock not given to a Carlyle recasting the French Revolution.

ROGER: [Laughing]

ORSON: And then be appalled that you're not writing your way through the French Revolution as fast as you expected.

ROGER: Poor Carlyle lost two years' work when a maid threw his manuscript into the fireplace.

ORSON: Two years' work lost, and he went straight home

and started to write it again. He was made of the sternest stuff. [Laughter] Those Goddamn Victorians had the capacity to write 5,000 words a day and dash off four or five long letters. I don't know how they did it. I spend hours and hours writing in my mind, not on paper, and I get it much better organized, but there's nothing to show for it.

ROGER: Have you tried dictating?

ORSON: No, no, I can't do that.

ROGER: You can't?

ORSON: I can do it, but it won't be of any value because I have entirely different instincts. I don't know what the motivating forces for your writing are. My whole instinct is to reduce to richness and smallness everything I want to say, and that takes even more time than your desire to write the history of the human race.

ROGER: True, but I don't have to take all my time trying to condense it. I mean, God, I'm not writing about the entire human race, just about one man's family. It's something I no longer have the facility to express without straining and changing and changing.

ORSON: Of course, the more you change, the longer it takes.

ROGER: Exactly.

ORSON: I'll call you soon.

ROGER: Bye.

[Lights dim.]

ACT ONE
SCENE FOUR

APRIL 3, 1983
"HAPPY BIRTHDAY TO ORSON FROM
THE TODD BOYS OF 1941"

Interior of Roger and Orson's libraries. Roger picks up telephone receiver and dials Orson. The telephone rings three times in Orson's dark library with no response, which activates his answering system.

ORSON: [Recorded message] Please leave a message. Orson.

ROGER: Orson, sorry I missed you. I've been thinking about your *Orson Welles Solo* project and your invitation for me to come out and continue our conversation on film. After our move from Florida, our files were scattered and it took me days to collect your stuff. Then, it occurred to me you should go over this before I come out for any further interviews. I'm still dubious about your contention that the public would be interested in your old schoolmaster, but your letter mentioning Ruth Gordon's autobiography, *My Side*, made me think that one of your *Solo* television programs featuring characters you've encountered over the decades would be saleable. Any interest in me, I think, will be as an antiquary, a vintage Victorian. This can easily be built up. I remember Victoria's death very well, and the special service conducted by my Canadian father. I remember the night bells rang out, not just for the old year, but, also, the old century. I remember the day my playmate, Leslie Bicerberger, got a phone call from his father, a high brass in the Army, saying he had been called to Washington because McKinley had been shot.

I remember as a child, learning about Edison's Kinetographic Theatre, better known as the Black Maria, where a number of the early short movies, lasting twenty to thirty seconds, were produced. A nickel would allow you to peer through a magnifying glass and see a snippet of a vaudeville act. But this call is mainly to ask where I should send your stuff. Sorry, I can't come out to work on *Rip* in the immediate future. I'm swamped with work on my revision of *Time and Chance,* but we'll talk about a date soon. As for your promised visit here, I have renewed hope, but little faith. It's time, long past time, to get together, either in your native Midwest, in Las Vegas, or in Los Angeles. We'll talk soon.

[Lights dim.]

[Interiors of Roger and Orson's libraries, May 6, 1983. Roger picks up telephone receiver and dials Orson. The telephone rings three times in Orson's dark library with no response, which activates his answering system.]

ORSON: [Recorded message] Please leave a message. Orson.

ROGER: [Roger leaves a phone message] Orson. Happy Birthday. Preceding you down life's highway by an exact twenty years, I find that each May I am a little surprised to still be among the quick, but delighted to be able to glance over a shoulder to be certain you are still maintaining the proper interval behind.

Like Prospero, I've recently been peering into the dark abysm of Time. I've begun delving into boxes of Todd files. I sort and I burn. I sort and I save. One item snatched from the burning was a letter I wrote you on your 30th birthday that reads in part:

May 7, 1945
My Beloved—

Today I looked at the calendar and was startled to realize that a momentous May date has come and gone. And was more startled to realize that your "twenties" had come and gone. And that—oh truly startling thought—my forties must therefore soon come faltering to an end. For we march eternally twenty annual paces apart…

By the time we have doubled the duration of our storied friendship, I will have reached the biblical allotment of three score and ten and you shall have reached my frightening—believe me—half century mark. We'll probably celebrate that momentous May with a rousing horseshoe match in St. Petersburg.

Until then, I continue in dauntless—if now treble-register—devotion.

R

That momentous date is long behind us and we've yet to play a game of horseshoes, rousing, or otherwise. Perhaps when I reach the century mark and you're a spry eighty we'll foregather for that long-postponed match. Another treasure is a scratchy old record bearing a label "Happy Birthday to Orson from the Todd Boys of 1941." I'll make a copy and send it to you, a rosemary for remembrance. Remembrance of that dear dead day, almost beyond recall, May 6, 1941, your twenty-sixth birthday, at the opening of *Kane*, when you and Dolores entered the theatre lobby, a quartet of Todd boys sang to the tune of *Happy Birthday to You* our altered lyrics. *Happy Birthday to you, /Felicitations we strew /On our dear friend Orson /From the boys old and new. /Let the Hearst face turn blue, /Shouting red bunk at you. /Those who know you, dear Orson /Know you're white through and through. /If he thinks Kane's like him, /It's his privilege and whim. /But if Kane's after Abel, /Why you're able to win. /So, we'll sing it once more /Though this tune's apt to bore. /Happy birthday, dear Orson, /Happy Birthdays galore.* I'll try reaching you later this evening.

[Lights dim.]

ACT ONE
SCENE FIVE

JUNE 20, 1983
AND DON'T IMAGINE THAT THIS RAGGLE-TAGGLE GYPSY-O IS CLAIMING TO BE FREE

Interior of Orson and Roger's libraries. Roger's telephone rings.

ROGER: Hello.

ORSON: Roger? Roger?

ROGER: Orson? My God, Welles, I was just writing to you to let you know when I will be arriving in Los Angeles.

ORSON: Wonderful! I know you're coming in on the twenty-second. What's the flight and time?

ROGER: United Flight 421, which is scheduled to arrive at 1:20 p.m.

ORSON: Great. I want to capture on film everything you mentioned on the answering machine the other day and more, lots more, but mostly I'm so looking forward to our long overdue visit. If I'm not tied up, Freddie [Gillette, Orson's driver] and I will meet you. I'll try to clear my calendar. I was just thinking of you. This morning, I viewed an hour's worth of documentary-in-progress featuring "Operation Sail" that took place seven years ago, when hundreds of tall ships from around the world converged in New York Harbor to celebrate America's 200th birthday. Your old friend, Irving

Johnson, was prominently featured. Looking at the film brought to mind my calling you and Hortense from California on that star-spangled day telling you of our plans to relocate back to America. Seeing the screen full of sails made me wax a bit nostalgic. I've never felt particularly sentimental about the Fourth of July except when I was younger than you ever knew me. When I was in Grand Detour, I used to see the old Gray and Blue guys marching along. That was the only thing that ever touched me. The tall ships got to me seven years ago. Seeing them again on this Fourth, touched me.

ROGER: Irving Johnson—

ORSON: Looked in great shape. But, you're equally amazing. You don't look eight-nine. [Roger laughs]

ROGER: Irving's an amazing guy. You're right; the flotilla of Tall Ships on the country's 200th anniversary was spectacular. The Fourth of July reminds me of sending you off to North Manitou Island, where you spent the Fourth working on our John Brown play, *Marching Song*. Remember that wild summer?

ORSON: I spent the Fourth with a gaggle of intoxicated and non-too-congenial Indians. Even when sober, of course, the noble Redman doesn't take too kindly to the Fourth of July.

ROGER: Oh, yes, and then you really had a time when you employed a few Indians to build a wigwam. It's still there, and has become a tourist attraction on what is now referred to as "Welles Point." I'm pretty sure I sent you a copy of that wonderful letter you wrote us from the Meigs place, updating your co-author on your playwriting efforts on our John Brown epic drama.

ORSON: I couldn't read it. I'm too old to read type that's on the head of a pin.

ROGER: I have the original here; let me read it to you. There's no date, but it's the summer of 1932 and you write:

[Center downstage behind a translucent scrim eighteen-year-old Orson takes a page out of a typewriter and reads his just completed letter.]

Dear Skip,

I've been away for three days now and haven't done a lick of work. But there! When I tell you where I am and why, you'll understand. The story begins with Mr. Meigs and it will persuade you that there is indeed a destiny, which shapes our ends. I met Bill and Jim Meigs' father recently and we talked at some length. He, it appears, maintains a summer establishment on Lake Flambeau in the Indian reservation. He said that between Mercer and Flambeau, there is no comparison. Would I stay on the train a few more miles and give Flambeau a trial. I certainly would. At Woodruff, a cross-eyed half-breed waited to take me to my reserved destination. It was six-thirty in the morning and he was raving drunk. I was glad to be able to refuse an eighteen-mile drive in his Model T Ford, very glad. And at Lac du Flambeau, that delightful capital of the Ojibwe Reservation, boasting a main street like an illustration from somebody's novel of life in the early lumbering and Indian-fighting days, there waiting, big and little, rose-faced and multitudinous: the Meigs. They drove me over miles of picturesque Chippewa trails, through pine forests and past myriad little lakes to their luxurious "Lodge," and here I was given as demoralizing a breakfast as has ever been fed to a co-dramatist. Later there was swimming—the water here is crystal and can be drunk with relish—and successively: sailing, in a snappy sloop that would put, I think, the old glitter in your seaman's eye, game fishing, Jim caught a muskie, sightseeing, Indian villages by motor-boat and Packard, and hunting, we went out for deer but brought home a brace of gamey partridge.

But need I go further? Need I say that when it developed that the reservation was as kind to my tortured nasal passages and be-spasmed bronchial tubes as anywhere South of the Fifty, it required only the opportunity to buy a wigwam and live in it in a pine grove a million miles from a telephone and another million to the next, solitudinous and—what pleases me most—entirely surrounded by water. Need I add that I have decided to stay? I am serious about the pine grove and the wigwam and lest I be accused of extravagance, let me state the entire arrangement is eminently economical. The pine grove, you see, is part of the Meigs estate and the wigwam which I have caused to be built by squaws and a few antiques of the neuter gender for the total reward of twenty-five fifty, gold, is something the Meigs have been long wanting. So by making the grand gesture of giving them it for their own for as long as birch-bark and rush mat shall remain incorporate (which, I am informed, is a matter of generations) I feel easy at accepting their hospitality— meals, that is, delicious meals, and camping materials de-lux. A wigwam or, more correctly, a wig-i-wam is emphatically a thing of the forest. It is fashioned of wild things; deer skin and bark, soft maple and basswood. Even the rope in the bulrush screening is of native manufacture. And being primitive and far removed from the high-pressure world of our civilization, its construction is a matter of time—exactly two days. So of course I haven't worked. The building of this great inverted salad bowl of a house of mine has been too fascinating a diversion. But tomorrow, tomorrow I shall roll up the proverbial sleeve and lay to. I have been so many centuries from John Brown and *Marching Song* during the past weekend that I rejoice in returning to it, to find my mind freshened and enthusiastic. If things go as promising as they began in this Utopia, I shall probably linger for the Autumnal turning of the leaves. Or what do you think? Love without end, Orson

[Lights dim.]

ORSON: Oh, that long-ago summer of youthful buoyancy and promise comes flooding back. Thank you.

ROGER: It's beautifully written. I want to include it in my chapter about you to point out how limpid and error free your adolescent letters were. They remind me of that line about Shakespeare's writing, "His mind and hand went together and what he thought, he uttered with such ease we have hardly received from him a blot in his papers."

ORSON: "We have scarce received."

ROGER: "Scarce received." Thank you, thank you, dear Orson.

ORSON: I always was a pedant. You're the one who taught me.

ROGER: And what was Ben Jonson's rejoinder, "Would that he had blotted a thousand."

ORSON: "The players have often mentioned it as an honor to Shakespeare that, in his writing, whatsoever is penned, he never blotted out a line. My answer hath been, 'Would that he have blotted a thousand.'" Yes, that's a great joke, I think. I don't know, I must have made what they call a fair copy because I'm a terrible changer. In the old days, people made time to write beautiful letters. Now, we don't have time for postcards. In my youth, people traveled at a slower place and had time to write thousands of words every week in beautiful language and script. How times have changed.

ROGER: We had a better education.

ORSON: You bet. That's the beginning of it, isn't it? Lately they've lowered the standards to such a degree that they've discovered vast multitudes of people toward the end of high school who can scarcely read. I listened to your recent phone message. Tell me more about your grandson's publishing venture.

ROGER: Hascy's son has been getting a lot of stuff published lately. He's a writer and photographer, and he has started his own publishing company. He's effective at attracting publicity. I'll send you a few pages the *Harvard Magazine* devoted to him. To cut the story short—

ORSON: Don't cut it short, I'm interested.

ROGER: One of his books is a collection of photographs and children's writing, sort of a *Family of Man* that focuses on children; it's a Family of Children, really. He's getting some backing and he wants to re-publish our books and sound recordings.

ORSON: Re-publish our books? By God, that's wonderful. Of course, I'm all for it. Keeping it in the family is great.

ROGER: The *Merchant* is absolutely spectacular because of your Shylock. To read the poet's words and simultaneously hear fine actors bring these to life produces ninety minutes of aesthetic delight. But we shouldn't gamble his dough on it because so many people, particularly Jewish people, continue to find Shylock objectionable.

ORSON: I keep going on the air doing, "Hath not a Jew eyes?" which makes Jewish people happy.

ROGER: I wrote an introduction to the second edition when we learned that *Merchant* was the least successful of our texts. I thought the problem with our first edition was a result of your ideas about how Shylock sneered at the Christians and

ridiculed their hypocrisy. But my introduction
didn't do any good. [Orson laughs] I don't think
he should spend his money to republish *Merchant*
first. Resistance to the play may limit its
marketability. He should begin by putting his
dough and time into *Caesar* alone. There's another
advantage to start with *Caesar*. It's not only the
most-taught school play; it's the one with the best
publicity possibilities. I mean plugs for the Welles
super-success on Broadway and the volumes of
critical praise available. Consider just one quote
from Robert Benchley which went about like this:
"Orson Welles and his Mercury Theatre give Julius
Caesar a reality which I think might fool the Bard
himself. It turns out there are two ways of doing
Shakespeare, the old way and the good way. By the
good way, I mean what Orson Welles is doing over
at the Mercury."

ORSON: He's bright and has ideas. He'll make a success, if
            not with our books, with other things.

ROGER: To expand, he needs more money like everybody
            else.

ORSON: It sounds to me like the tribulations of an up and
            coming publisher.

ROGER: He prefers being self-employed to being a wage
            slave.

ORSON: He needs to be self-employed and that means being
            a capitalist. He needs to be an impossible boss
            rather than an impossible employee. Are his books
            selling?

ROGER: Fairly well. Harcourt Brace is interested in marketing
            and distributing them. If he agrees to this, he

Design by Emil Orlick in a Rhinehardt production

RECORD 3

ACT I

Scene III

VENICE—A Public Place

There are countless arrangements for this scene, but many of the most successful settings have employed these elements: a little square with a fountain or a well in the center; to one side Shylock's house, or a part of it, showing the door and a window above. Running along the back is a canal with other buildings visible beyond. Also, if possible, because it has been found tremendously effective in stage-business, a bridge. Shylock, instead of entering after the curtain has risen, might be "discovered" either at his door, or at the top of this bridge. Bassanio, who stands near him, has obviously just been asking, in Antonio's name, for the loan of some money. The old Jew is regarding him shrewdly. Out of the bearded face, cut with hard wrinkles, peer glittering black eyes, surprisingly keen.

WALTER HAMPDEN SHYLOCK

From _The Mercury Shakespeare_ (formerly _Everybody's Shakespeare_) _The Merchant of Venice_ with a sample of Orson's adroit illustrations.

would give up control to a certain extent. He would like to run it himself. But, I don't think he's got the capital to do it.

ORSON: I understand his problem. [Roger laughs] I'd like to run it myself, but I don't have the capital. That's the story of my life. It's hard to be self-employed nowadays. It's a very small minority who don't belong to an immense bureaucracy. The family grocery store owner, the individual publisher, the independent filmmaker—we're all dinosaurs.

ROGER: Mavericks certainly, which you addressed so well in your Lifetime Achievement Award remarks.

[Center downstage behind a translucent scrim, Orson delivers his 1975 American Film Institute Lifetime Achievement Award address.]

My father once told me that the art of receiving a compliment is of all things the sign of a civilized man. And he died soon afterwards, leaving my education in this important matter sadly incomplete. I'm only sad that on this, the occasion of the rarest compliment he ever could have dreamed of, that he isn't here to see his son so publicly at a loss.

In receiving a compliment—or trying to—the words are all worn out by now. They're polluted by ham and corn and when you try to scratch around for some new ones, it's just an exercise in empty cleverness. What I feel this evening is not very clever. It's the very opposite of emptiness. The corny old phrase is the only one I know to say it.

My heart is full. With a full heart—with all of it—I thank you.

This is Samuel Johnson on the subject of what he calls "Contrarieties."

"There are goods so opposed that we cannot seize both, and in trying, fail to seize either. Flatter not yourself," he says, "with contrarieties. Of the blessings set before you, make your choice. No man can at the same time fill his cup from the source and from the mouth of the Nile."

Well, this business of contrarieties has to do with us. With you who are paying me this compliment and with me who has strayed so far from this hometown of ours. Not that I'm alone in this, or unique. I am never that. But there are a few of us left in this conglomerated world of ours who still trudge stubbornly along the lonely, rocky road and this is, in fact, our contrariety.

We don't move nearly as fast as our cousins on the freeway. We don't even get as much accomplished, just as the family-sized farm can't possibly raise as many crops or get as much profit as the agricultural factory of today.

What we do come up with has no special right to call itself better. It's just different. No, if there's any excuse for us at all it's that we're simply following the old American tradition of the maverick. And we are a vanishing breed. This honor I can only accept in the name of all the mavericks. And also as a tribute to the generosity of all the rest of you—to the givers—to the ones with fixed addresses.

A maverick may go his own way but he doesn't think that it's the only way or even that it's the best one—except maybe for himself. And don't imagine that this raggle-taggle gypsy-o is claiming to be free. It's just that some of the necessities to which I am a slave are different from yours.

As a director, for instance, I pay myself out of my acting jobs. I use my own work to subsidize my work. In other words, I'm crazy. But not crazy enough to pretend to be free. But it's a fact that many of the films you've seen tonight could never have been made otherwise. Or if otherwise—well, they might have been better. But certainly they wouldn't have been mine. The truth is I don't believe that this great evening would ever have brightened my life if it weren't for this—my own particular contrariety.

Let us raise our cups, then standing, as some of us do, on opposite ends of the river and drink together to what really matters to us all—to our crazy and beloved profession. To the movies—to good movies—to every possible kind.

I leave you now in default of the eloquence this high occasion deserves with another very short scene from the same film—a piece of which you saw earlier with John Huston and Peter Bogdanovich— just by way of saying good night from one who will remember tonight—not as a sort of gala visit, but as a very happy homecoming. And who remains not only your obedient servant, but also in this age of supermarkets, your friendly neighborhood grocery store. Good night. Thank you.

[Lights dim.]

ROGER: How are things with you?

ORSON: I've shot a twenty-minute segment of what I'm calling *The Magic Show*, where I play the part of an aging magician, a pompous old-time conjurer doing all the big tricks in the middle of his act, but he's losing his memory, and he can't remember how anything works. He forgets how to put the woman back together, or to bring the floating lady down. He's led away and the theatre is empty. Then a rousing number of Keystone Kops come in and discover the woman sawed in half, the other lady floating in air, as well as a number of other illusions only partially completed, and they valiantly try to complete them. Throughout this segment, there's no dialogue. In a bow to the silent movies, there'll be musical accompaniment and title cards.

ROGER: An amnesiac magician. It sounds clever and poignant.

ORSON: That's only one segment of this expansive romp and rumination on the history and charisma of magic. I open the show with a wisp of nostalgia. "There was a time in our country," I inform the audience, "when every whistle stop had a live theatre of its own. We are about to take you to those grand old days when we magicians did our stuff in gilded palaces, sumptuously upholstered in scarlet plush and purple hokum."

ROGER: Charming. How much of Houdini will you include?

ORSON: You can't ignore a giant, and he will receive the proper homage due. But, I also want to comment on other talented and colorful characters that comprise the pantheon of magician legends, such as William Robinson, who conned the world into believing he was the magnificent Chinese magician, Chung Ling Soo.

ROGER: How did he manage that piece of legerdemain?

ORSON: He was a brilliant con man, who billed himself as "the Original Chinese Conjurer." Offstage, he maintained his stage persona. When he granted interviews, he brought along an interpreter, claiming he didn't speak English. Robinson was impressed by the dazzling work of a contemporary Chinese magician, Ching Ling Foo. In addition to breathing fire, Foo brought forth from his mouth a fifteen-foot pole, and then, waving a cloth in the air, brought forth a vast bowl of water and plucked out a child.

The inevitable happened and both magicians found themselves performing in London, Ching Ling Soo at the Hippodrome Theatre and Foo on another stage in the same block. They both billed themselves as "The Original Chinese Conjurer," and their mutual animus made front-page news. Ultimately, Ching Ling Foo offered 1,000 pounds to Soo if he could perform ten of Foo's twenty tricks. A date and time for the competition was arranged. The moment arrived and so did Soo, but no Foo, which led to more controversy and lively headlines. One classic headline read something like, "Did Foo Fool Soo and Should Soo Sue Foo?" Robinson went on to a long and successful career until 1918, when he was accidentally shot on stage performing the bullet catch, where a marksman fired bullets and the magician would catch them in his teeth. He died the next day, which was, ironically, Houdini's birthday. After I recount Robinson's tragic end, I perform the bullet trick.

ROGER: You don't know when it's going to be on?

ORSON: No. A good deal of work remains to be completed before it's ready to be aired.

ROGER: You said something about going back to Paris?

ORSON: Yes, and I'm not going. I decided it's not worth the expense and the effort at this stage. I've been spending more time at the Lancaster Hotel in Paris, attempting to arrange financing and gain possession of *The Other Side of the Wind,* than here in Los Angeles. I'm given promises and told to wait and wait and wait. I received more promises at this year's Cannes Film Festival. I'm staying here for now. I've got enough work here, so it's better to stay and make some money.

ROGER: I worry about you when you travel because I don't
             think you should go alone.

ORSON: Are you ready to put earth around my grave?

ROGER: [Laughing] No. No. No. But, it's ridiculous for you
             to travel alone.

ORSON: Well, you're traveling alone to come see me. We
             both may be battered, but unbowed and able to
             board and unboard a plane. You say you're old.
             Are you in pain?

ROGER: No. It's just—

ORSON: Old age?

ROGER: I'm as old as your friend, George Burns.

ORSON: George said to me the other day, rather poignantly,
             "I've only got one contemporary friend left
             alive."

ROGER: The last of my college crowd, Sam Raphaelson,
             died several years ago. We founded the Lambkins
             Society for student playwrights, actors, and
             composers. Raph was the most talented and the
             most modest of our group.

ORSON: He was a very good writer. Lubitsch was the greatest
             master of high comedy in the history of movies.
             You look at the Lubitsch movies and you see that
             your friend, Raphaelson, wrote every one of the
             great ones. Raphaelson's scripts had a lot to do
             with those successes. He had a very distinguished
             career. When one thinks of him, one usually
             remembers *The Jazz Singer*. That's only one of
             many triumphs.

ROGER: He was a frequent contributor when I was editor
           of the university humor magazine, *The Asylum*. At
           that time, he had a bureau drawer full of rejection
           slips, and *The Jazz Singer* was one of them.

ORSON: Persistence is often its own reward. Before I sign
           off, I want to mention Henry Hudson in some-
           thing I'm writing. What do you know about him?
           He, like a gaggle of others, was looking for a passage
           to the Orient, but I don't recall the particulars.

ROGER: If memory serves, he was obsessed with discovering
           an all-water northwest passage to Asia. He sailed
           his *Half Moon* from Amsterdam, landed on the
           coast of Maine, and sailed south to the Chesapeake
           and Delaware Bays. Neither appeared to be the
           entrance to the passage to the Orient. Then this
           intrepid character sailed north to the mouth of the
           river that today bears his name, and spent a good
           deal of time exploring it.

ORSON: Was this about 1600, or a little later?

ROGER: You flatter me to ask. I would guess about that
           date, maybe a decade later.

ORSON: Something made getting to the Indies important
           at about that time. Everybody made their heroic
           sails and I've forgotten what it is, the discovery
           of pepper in West Sussex or something. Oh, I
           know what it was, the collapse of the Venetian
           Empire in the lower Balkans and Turkey, which
           depressed the high prices that the Ottomans were
           demanding for their spices. That old Doge, Enrico
           Dandolo, who was eighty-seven years old and
           blind, led the victorious battle. He must have
           been quite a fellow.

ROGER: That I didn't know.

ORSON: You know a lot more than I do and I keep reading history all the time. I have great trouble connecting things. It's been true all my life. That very bad mural I painted on the walls of Rogers Hall, I discovered, many years later in horror, had ended up as the ceiling for the elementary students' playhouse, known as Shantytown.

ROGER: Shantytown? Oh, yes.

ORSON: It was an attempt to place some historic notables together in a time sequence.

ROGER: It was wonderful. You had a phenomenal grasp of world history.

ORSON: Recorded history—our brilliant, idiotic, and transcendent struggle out of the cave, fascinated me at Todd and still does. But I have a little trouble between the fifteenth and the end of the seventeenth century. I realize now why you learn dates in history. Without a sense of time, it's impossible to appreciate who were the contemporaries of Peter the Great, or Catherine the Great.

ROGER: Tie them in with your literary figures.

ORSON: What literary figures?

ROGER: Shakespeare for God's sakes.

ORSON: Shakespeare was a contemporary of Peter the Great? Really? While he was building that iron foundry in Petrozavodsk, Shakespeare was writing plays?

"That very bad mural I painted on the walls of Rogers Hall," at age twelve.

ROGER: Near contemporaries.

ORSON: I thought Shakespeare had been dead for more
than fifty years when Peter the Great was born. I've
seen pictures of Peter the Great with pigtails. I've
never seen pictures of anybody in Elizabethan
England in pigtails. So, he must have come upon
the scene later than Shakespeare.

ROGER: Near contemporaries is a relative term.

ORSON: I take a more literal view. It isn't right to say he's a
contemporary of Shakespeare. They were several
generations removed. Peter wore entirely different
clothes than Will.

ROGER: True.

ORSON: Nobody wore anything like that until Shakespeare
had been dead for twenty years. What's amazing is
how fast the styles changed until recently. Look at
a photograph taken in 1915 when I was born.
Men's clothing, except for the collar and a very
slight difference in the tailoring, is exactly the same
as today. For one glorious moment, everybody
broke out with Nehru jackets. Now it's blue jeans,
but when dressing up, men still look basically like
Warren G. Harding.

ROGER: [Laughs] You're right. All the changes have been in women's fashions.

ORSON: Our reluctance to alter our clothing is particularly striking when you think that during the thirteenth century, within a period of twelve years, all Europe changed its fashion. It's also fascinating to me how quickly information was transmitted during this period, which led to a number of rapid changes throughout Europe. How did the news spread so quickly?

ROGER: How, indeed?

ORSON: And it did. I suppose a major motivator was curiosity, which is kind of marvelous.

ROGER: I can't even speculate about communications in the thirteenth century. But, in the early 1850s, my grandfather, John Almanza Rowley Rogers, co-founder of Berea College, was a preacher in southwestern Illinois. His diary talks about going to preach twenty and thirty miles away and returning the same day. That truly amazes me.

ORSON: He must have been an early riser. Instead of being provincial and closed, as you might think our forefathers were, most had a good idea of what was happening in Moscow and Paris and in Madrid, and that's wonderful. Of course, they wrote each other letters that never ended. Nobody will explain to me where they got the time to dip their pen in ink and rub it with sand and write two thousand words a day.

ROGER: That's right. Now, you need to sharpen your quill and begin your memoir.

ORSON: Yes, when *Lear* is completed, I'll begin in earnest. Did I tell you that Swifty Lazar, a literary agent, contacted me a year ago?

ROGER: You mentioned several publishers that are interested in publishing your memoir.

ORSON: Knopf is the most persistent. They have been after me for years to write about my tattered life.

ROGER: Your reflections in *Paris Vogue* last year are a great start. Keep your quill busy.

ORSON: Speaking of quills, I was persuaded to use a quill for a while. A lady friend who was a poetess, countess, and grande dame in France wrote all her books with a quill.

ROGER: Really?

ORSON: She taught me how to use them. It is a very pleasant way to write in longhand. Frighteningly enough, you kind of like it.

ROGER: Goose quills?

ORSON: Goose quills, which reminds me of a great line from a Middle West film distributor in the thirties who sent a telegram to the home office in Hollywood saying, "Don't send us no more of those pictures where the leading man signs his name with a feather." That kind of sums up all the travel movies. Did I tell you I bought a program the other day from *Girl of the Golden West*?

ROGER: No.

ORSON: It was a David Belasco play that opened in New

York. I'm going to give it to Keenan Wynn because his grandfather, Frank Keenan, was one of the stars in it. Frank, the father of Ed Wynn, played the villain. I thought Keenan would like to see it. My God, it opened in 1905, and the program looks like it's fifty years before I possibly could have been born, when it was only a decade. All the ads, the women's clothes, the language, and everything are antiquities that send shivers down my spine.

ROGER: Change is so rapid.

ORSON: And not always for the better. The covers of *Time* and *Newsweek* have become so sleazy. They used to be very elegant. Remember when *Time* always had a portrait?

ROGER: A portrait in a frame, yes, and I remember your 1938 portrait best of all, which makes me think of your old Mercury Theatre pal, Chubby Sherman.

ORSON: You've heard about Chubby Sherman recently?

ROGER: No.

ORSON: His mind is gone. He's insane.

ROGER: Really?

ORSON: Yes, babbling of green fields.

ROGER: Oh, God.

ORSON: His ten-year bout with mental illness, like all tragedy, teeters on the edge of farce. He's now back in his ancestral home in Springfield, Illinois, and driving all his cousins mad. They're threatening to take him off to the laughing academy. He's come to a pitiful end.

ROGER: Losing one's mind is another pitfall of growing old. Old age has few advantages, and the prospect of senility isn't one of them.

ORSON: Senility is not what's bothering poor Chubby. He suffers from mental illness. He's loony. Loony isn't senile. You're not going to sit around the lunch table and set fire to your napkin. [Roger chuckles] Stop confusing the loss of your faculties with going bananas. They are two quite distinct rocky roads.

ROGER: Do you realize that we have so many friends that have known tragedy?

ORSON: Tragedy is a very common human condition.

ROGER: That's right. It always seemed to me that Chubby's leaving the Mercury was the reason for its demise. You were so high on him and, all of a sudden, he called you on the phone and said he wanted to make more money somewhere else.

ORSON: Yes, he had a good play where he could get a bigger salary. I didn't have a major part for him then, so it was a natural thing to do.

ROGER: Yes, but I remember your phone call and you were pretty—

ORSON: Upset.

ROGER: Upset. Of course, we all have simplistic answers, but it seemed to me that Chubby killed the Mercury.

ORSON: I don't really think so because the Mercury went on to Hollywood fame.

ROGER: No, I mean the Mercury Theatre.

ORSON: The Mercury Theatre was killed by lack of funds and our subsequent move to Hollywood. All the money I had made on radio was spent on the Mercury, but I didn't make enough money to finance the entire operation. Hollywood was really the only choice. It wasn't because of Chubby leaving. I think all acting companies have a lifespan. The Mercury Theatre came to an end. My partnership with John Houseman came to an end with the move to California. He became my employee, expensive, and not terribly pleasant or productive. Our mutual discomfort led to his decamping California and returning to New York. For years, Virginia [Orson's first wife] warned me that Houseman would be my Iago. For a long time, I didn't want to believe her, but she was right. He became consumed with jealousy and has spent a lifetime since painting me as the villain in the piece.

ROGER: Oh, sure, there are two sides to—

ORSON: *There's* a real Roger adage.

ROGER: [Laughs] That's right, there are two sides to every argument, for Christ's sake.

ORSON: There should never be another side to a friend's argument.

ROGER: That's true, and yours is the side of the angels. Friends and tragedy bring to mind Virginia's second husband, and your boon companion,

Charlie Lederer. What a talented screenwriter and blithe spirit he was.

ORSON: Wonderful Charlie. He was afflicted with crippling rheumatoid arthritis, and he compounded the problem by becoming a terrible doper and killing himself with it.

ROGER: It started by his taking pain-killing drugs? Lederer was an alcoholic?

ORSON: Charlie was always a heavy drinker, but no, what ruined him were drugs. He was bent over almost double with pain, and that led him to dope. It was a very unpleasant change in personality. His dear friend, Ben Hecht became furious with Charlie because he was walking around, going to parties, and kind of showing off what a wreck he was. All of us who knew and cared about him were very pained.

ROGER: I didn't think Charlie was old enough to be a pal of Ben Hecht's.

ORSON: They were very close. They wrote a number of famous movies together. Charlie was about fifteen years younger than Hecht, and he was a great talent. In the old days, because of Charlie's youth, he was sort of a mascot to all those old-timers who were twenty or thirty years older. When Ben Hecht would sign to do three movies, which he couldn't possibly finish in a month, Charlie would write two of them. He was also pretty close to Charlie MacArthur. Charlie came to me shortly before he died and pleaded that he could get some much needed money by providing the photographs for Marion Davies' autobiography, *The Times We Had*, but he said, the only way to get the book published, was if I would write the introduction. So I wrote an introduction praising Marion Davies, and it got published. It was sad that having the book published was a big event for Charlie.

ROGER: I thought after Marion Davies died that Charlie would come into money and things would be easy for him.

ORSON: No, he was left a house, and not much of anything else. He had to go right on earning his own living, and sadly, making unfortunate choices. I was playing in Las Vegas and Charlie came to see me. Afterwards, we went to a casino and he lost $28,000 at craps in about fifteen minutes. He had to work for over a year to pay it back. But before the world caved in on him, what a delight he was. In the late '40s and early '50s, between films, when Charlie was around, we devoted more time than we should have engaging in practical jokes.

ROGER: He was a great practical joker.

ORSON: You were a partner in crime with him on more than one occasion.

ROGER: One vivid memory was his outrage at a restricted country club in Los Angeles. He commandeered a riding lawnmower, took me along, and proceeded to cut the word SHIT on the first green. It left an indelible impression when members of the club arrived the next morning, the opening day of a celebrity tournament.

ORSON: Yes, it was a golf club that wouldn't allow Jews. I have forgotten all the details, but I know it involved you and Charlie.

ROGER: We sneaked out at night and were lucky we didn't end up in jail.

ORSON: A nationally recognized educator involved in a Hollywood scandal.

ROGER: That was taking a chance. The other thing that might have ruined an educator's reputation was during your early days in New York. Alex Woollcott, who was very big on you, wrote one of his best lines in the telegram he sent you after your *War of the Worlds* broadcast. It read something like "This only goes to prove, my beamish boy, that the intelligent people were all listening to a dummy, and all the dummies were listening to you." According to Houseman, Woollcott broadcast around town that, "Orson Welles and his great good friend, his boarding school headmaster, was a frequent visitor," never acknowledging Horty's presence.

ORSON: Of course, we all knew what that means!

ROGER: Especially with the Woollcott crowd. [Great laughter] God knows you and Charlie cut a caper or two.

ORSON: Didn't we just? Chicken pox precipitated one of our more memorable escapades. Two brothers who were producers were always in my hair. I was staying at the Waldorf Towers on my way to Europe. Several days before, I had picked up a case of the chicken pox from Chrissy [Christopher Welles Feder, Orson and Virginia's daughter] when I stopped off at Todd. By the time I arrived in New York, I had passed the point where I was contagious, but I was still speckled like a leper. The two producers invited themselves to my suite, and then Charlie, who happened to be in town, arrived and I introduced him as Dr. Gottlieb from the Port Authority. Charlie immediately declared the suite of rooms in the Waldorf in quarantine with no one being allowed to leave for a week. The brothers became hysterical. We kept them there for two days and nights. The doctor kept arriving in what appeared to be an increasingly drunken condition, and gave them injections of water. Charlie finally showed up, stumbling around flailing a needle that was bent in three directions. By this time, the producers were climbing the walls.

ROGER: [Laughing]

ORSON: I couldn't have done it without Charlie as the doctor. As time went on, we tried to keep the co-captives' spirits up by playing music and telling them how relatively few people died from this disease, no more than 47 percent of the people who were exposed. [Laughter] It was a happy time. I've forgotten their names. They were the kind of people who would believe anything. We had room service and kept the waiters at a distance. The brothers were sobbing at one point, sobbing tears. It was wonderful talking with you, and I'll see you soon.

ROGER: You're so wonderful to call. Do you realize we haven't seen each other since you invited me to share the stage with you at the American Film Institute's *Working with Welles* five years ago?

ORSON: It's been far too long. I feel cheated and hobbled when I'm not in your presence.

ROGER: Every reunion is a cause for great joy. But I wonder if this is the right time, given your herculean schedule and my writing projects that are behind schedule.

ORSON: There will be time for both of us to work and time to enjoy one another's company. I'm going to be dead soon. You'd better hurry and board that plane.

ROGER: I see your flair for the dramatic hasn't diminished. You've convinced me, though it didn't take much convincing, that the time for reunion is long overdue.

ORSON: It will be so good to see you.

ROGER: It will indeed. Bye.

ORSON: Bye.

[Lights dim.]

ACT ONE
SCENE SIX

JULY 21, 1983
HOW MANY PEOPLE YOUR AGE HAVE LOVING
FRIENDS AND BUMBLING OLD ACQUAINTANCES?

Mid-afternoon, interior of the foyer and library of Orson's Los Angeles home. Doorbell rings. Orson extricates himself from behind the desk in his library and walks to the front door, flings it open and warmly embraces Roger before his guest has an opportunity to rid himself of the two bags he is carrying. After the untangling of arms and suitcases, Orson ushers Roger into his library. Despite being twenty years Orson's senior, Roger is the far more animated of the two. Both seat themselves, Roger in a large leather chair, and Orson on a couch facing Roger. Between them is a large glass coffee table, on top of which rests a large bowl of fruit, two glasses, and an ice bucket containing bottled water. Several times during this scene, Roger will get up from his seat and pace energetically about the library, a lifelong means of dissipating his boundless energy.

ORSON: *[After greeting Roger, Orson shuts the front door as he calls out to Freddie.]* Thank you, Freddie. I'll call you later this afternoon about our schedule for tomorrow. Would you call Gary and see what his availability is for tomorrow? *[The sound of an automobile starting and leaving with dispatch. Orson shuts the door and addresses Roger.]* Faithful Freddie joyfully marches to his own hyperactive drummer. He's wonderfully dependable when you can catch him. Why do you insist on carrying your bags when Freddie volunteered to bring them in?

ROGER: Vanity. Plus poor Freddie's done enough heavy lifting for the day by bringing me here safely from the airport. You can't pay him too much for squiring you around this town. The horrific traffic snarl out here lives up to its reputation. Let me drop my bags in the guest room. [*Roger departs to the guest room and Orson walks to the kitchen. Moments later, Roger returns to the empty library and sits down in a large captain's chair. Orson returns pushing a wheeled groaning board brimming with sandwiches, platters containing samples of international cuisine as well as fruit, assorted desserts, and several carafes of wine.*]

ORSON: Yes, the constant congestion on the expressways has led to an epidemic of road rage. I've never relished driving and haven't driven since I wrapped one of your cars around a tree in my callow youth. Out here, I wouldn't. Thank God, Freddie is not so disinclined. Did they feed you on the plane?

ROGER: They offered, but I wasn't hungry.

ORSON: So, you haven't had anything to eat since leaving Chicago?

ROGER: Two Hershey bars.

ORSON: You've been subsisting on Hershey bars and Lifesavers ever since I've known you. You have no shame.

ROGER: None.

ORSON: I thought you might not have eaten, so I had Freddie go out this morning and bring back a wide sampling for us—from sweet and sour pork to chicken enchiladas, corned beef to lobster. Help yourself. [*Orson wheels the food-laden cart close to Roger.*]

ROGER: A feast worthy of Falstaff. A groaning board truly
           worthy of the name. [*Orson gathers a full plate of
           food and sits down. Roger's portion is much more
           modest.*]

ORSON: Don't make me eat alone. Put something of substance
           on your plate. Try a lobster, have some roast beef.
           Eat.

ROGER: [*Rises and walks over to the table of food and gingerly
           adds to his plate and returns to his seat.*] On the
           phone last night, when I asked you about *Lear*,
           you were evasive.

ORSON: I wasn't evasive. It's just a painful subject and I
           didn't want to dwell on it.

ROGER: When we spoke last week, you were optimistic that
           funding for the project was at hand.

ORSON: That was last week, and it did appear that I'd finally
           procured backing. Yesterday, the deal collapsed. At
           just the moment I was convinced all the brass balls
           were juggling perfectly, they dissolved into soap
           bubbles.

ROGER: Oh, God, another blow. Is there any correlation
           between this dour news and the chipped tooth
           that's causing you agony?

ORSON: No, the chipped tooth isn't the result of any gnashing
           of teeth. It just broke apart. The tooth just hurts,
           but the cratered financing is devastating. On top of
           all this, in recent weeks, I've been sword dancing
           with a young director who talks and talks and talks
           about his "vision" for a film that he may or may
           not direct and coyly dangles the possibility of a
           lucrative acting job in front of me. Yesterday, I was

told through an intermediary that the project is off. My last few days make the last act of *Camille* look like a comedy. No, more like a French farce, a Feydeau.

ROGER: No wonder you look exhausted. You take on too much. I keep encouraging you to write and to lecture. You can't top *Kane*. Focus your great talent in other directions.

ORSON: I can do both, and while I'm still able to make pictures, I want to remain in the game, my own game.

ROGER: Well, you're still young and maybe you can damn well top *Kane* and write.

ORSON: It's not a matter of topping *Kane*; it's just that there are so many pictures in my head that I want to put on film. And, no, I'm only young in your eyes. I'm a relic, but strangely I feel young, and, until the last few days, full of energy.

ROGER: I've felt young all my life. It's only since Horty died that I've begun to feel old. I look in the mirror and my feeling is confirmed. But, to use a favorite phrase of yours, "Considering the alternative."

ORSON: I'm glad you're going to get a second opinion on the buzzing in your ears while you're out here. I suffer all the time and keep my pains to my doctor and myself.

ROGER: You're remarkably stoic.

ORSON: So, you're not Tarzan of the Apes. If the buzzing in your ears isn't life threatening, it will be just another of life's annoyances you tolerate.

ROGER: I don't think I could stand great physical pain. Mine is mostly mental pain, if that's the proper word for growing old.

ORSON: How many people your age have loving friends and bumbling old acquaintances?

ROGER: Oh, you are absolutely right.

ORSON: Well then, where's your kick? [Chuckles]

ROGER: I haven't got any right to kick. [Laughing] Well, let me give you a comment on old age. Coming up in a day or two we will have an eclipse of the sun and that got me thinking that Halley's Comet is returning in 1986.

ORSON: Yes.

ROGER: It reminds me that when I was a senior at Todd, in 1910, I had an amazing teacher, a real eccentric character, C.Z. Aughenbaugh. Before your day, Todd had a mammoth, communal outdoor john, an eight-holer to be exact. No, not the Chic Sale type. We had a building east of Clover, which boasted a fine row of urinals, graduated in height, facing eight lattice-door stalls for serious elimination. After breakfast, the use of this facility, for boys and male faculty alike, was a queue-up affair. One patron alone, the great Seezy, knew no waiting and heard no imprecations to hurry. It was his privilege and his pleasure to spend the entire period between breakfast and Chapel, or so it seems in retrospect, informing, prophesying, and pontificating on his Delphic throne in that reserved No. 1 stall. I learned of Queen Victoria's demise while sitting three doors north of our mentor. Tolstoy's too. Ask me about the Boxer Rebellion. Or the Russo-

Japanese War. My knowledge is considerable and all flavored with the pungent aroma of that strange seminar.

ORSON: What made him an inspiring teacher?

ROGER: He was bursting with a top teacher's prime requirement, contagious enthusiasm. Seezy was a vivid, glowing character. In a too-often colorless profession, this man stood out like Mars at Perihelion. On the day Halley's Comet was to make its appearance, he got us up before dawn, a little before four o'clock in the morning, to see it. It was a tremendous thing that spread across the sky that long ago evening.

ORSON: Great.

ROGER: I remember him saying, "There'll probably be one or two of you alive when it comes the next time." And he added, "My guess is Roger, who's the son of a family that lives forever." My father's mother was then about 100.

ORSON: Yes.

ROGER: Now, I've established a deadline. I'm going be with you, and I'll quit talking about my troubles until after Halley's Comet returns in 1986.

ORSON: So, you're going to make the next Halley's Comet. Well, I'll get off my chair and I'll be with you.

ROGER: That's a date. I'm confident I'll make it even though I'm a generation behind you.

ORSON: A generation? What are you talking about? Four generations. [Burst of laughter] You can remember when the first electric lights stretched out on the horizon.

ROGER: But, you have such an ability to go back in history that I seldom get ahead of you on anything.

ORSON: My recall of the past is very patchy. World War II has been on my mind of late. I may narrate a documentary on the subject. I remember vividly being chilled to my bones by the thought that the Nazis had bombed the open city of Guernica in 1937, a cultural and religious center, which had no military defenses. Three-quarters of the town of 15,000 was leveled, and 1,500 died. Only a few years later, we were applauding our own bombardiers, who killed tens of thousands of people, more dead than either Hiroshima or Nagasaki in Dresden, a city of little war-related importance. It was a cultural center, with the magnificent Zwinger Palace, the Dresden State Opera House, and the Frauenkirche Church of our Lady. Dresden was called "Elbflorenz," the Florence of the Elbe. The bombings were ordered, in large part, to intimidate the Russians, to let them know what American and British bombers could accomplish.

ROGER: Yes, and that was Truman's argument to end the war with Japan by dropping atomic bombs on Hiroshima and Nagasaki.

ORSON: Japan was about to drop to its knees before it happened. And there was already a peace party.

ROGER: In Japan?

ORSON: In Japan, before the bomb, the Prime Minister himself and a whole lot of people in his group were saying, "Let's surrender as long as we can keep our

Emperor." And Truman said, "The hell with the Emperor, we demand unconditional surrender." I never agreed with dropping the bomb, but understood his decision, which ended the war and prevented continuing misery. The bombs certainly brought Japan to its knees.

ROGER: I was all starry-eyed. You were, too. We thought that we could make a world government that would work.

ORSON: After covering the United Nations Conference on International Organization, in San Francisco, for the *New York Post* and my weekly radio program, *The Free World Forum*, I remember driving to the airport after witnessing and reporting on the founding charter of the United Nations that established "equal rights for large and small nations," thinking that the starry-eyed days were over. Even then you could see that the lines were drawn between the east and west. You could see from the Russians that there was no hope of a dialogue. I went to San Francisco starry-eyed as you say, but I left pretty much the realist I've remained ever since. We are the only animal on earth bent on destroying ourselves. Since Los Alamos, we've had the weapons to do so. The question for our age, and all ages that follow, is how are we going to handle this destructive urge?

ROGER: Do you hold out much hope for the future?

ORSON: I'm not without hope. We must live in hope, or else why bother to live? But it's hard for me to be very optimistic at this point.

ROGER: I'm close to finishing my book on the making of

Rip Van Winkle Renascent, and my argument for
promoting global peace. The movie had a gala
opening in 1948, with, among others, Eleanor
Roosevelt in attendance, at New York's Museum
of Modern Art. Jock Whitney, whose money
built MOMA as well as the Whitney Museum,
hosted the event. Weeks before, I was at a party in
New York and showed the just completed film to
Todd alumni and friends. Jock Whitney was there
and was generous in his praise. We had lunch the
next day, where he arranged the MOMA reception
and showing of *Rip*.

ORSON: At the Museum of Modern Art?

ROGER: Yes. It was all a matter of luck. Jock just happened
to be at this party. Horty was with you in Europe.
It was Thanksgiving vacation, and I'd brought
Chris to New York to visit her new stepfather,
Pringle, who would then take her to his home in
South Africa.

ORSON: You're right. It was lucky that Jock saw the film.
I was quite fond of him.

ROGER: You must have met him because of his interest in
films.

ORSON: Met him? I knew him very well.

ROGER: He had a close connection with Selznick, didn't he?

ORSON: No, he only financed Selznick. He's never been in
the movies. I got to know Jock very well when he
was ambassador to England. He used to invite me
to dinner all the time and I also knew Sunny
Whitney equally well. Over dinner one evening in
London, Jock went on at length about his fond

memories as a student at Yale, where he was the stroke of the school's crew his last two years. One afternoon, early in his rowing career, he entered a New Haven barbershop and requested a "Hindenburg" military cut to reduce wind resistance and improve his time. Mind you, he was in school during the mid-'20s, shortly after the war, and the barber recommended he consider calling it another name. In homage to the team, Jock christened it the "crew cut."

ROGER: He told me that he started Pioneer Pictures.

ORSON: Yes, he formed the company that financed *Gone With the Wind*, and that was a pretty lucky piece of financing as you can well imagine. He then thought he'd become a movie mogul. But, he was too canny. The Whitneys were too smart to put money into movies. Having hit it big as he did with *Gone With the Wind*, and a couple of others, *Rebecca* and *A Star is Born*, he moved that dough right over to something more reliable, such as Minute Maid Orange Juice. He was also a generous contributor to the arts. Sadly, few individual investors put money into the arts as tax shelters and write-offs. Jock was old money with a sense of obligation to the community. He, like many in the old money fraternity, thought you had to do something; you had to contribute to the arts.

ROGER: Where did the original money come from?

ORSON: It's four or five generations old. It was banking money in the beginning.

ROGER: Later, the family invested in railroads.

ORSON: Jock's paternal grandfather was an early crony of one of the biggest crooks in American history, old man Rockefeller.

ROGER: Rockefeller was certainly an original, an unscrupulous titan of industry, a devout Baptist, an advocate of temperance, a complicated psalm singing, *Bible*-thumping Standard Oil brigand, who was also the biggest philanthropist of his day.

ORSON: His was the era when moguls were real pirates because there was no legislation to stop them from doing anything. My first job in commercial radio was playing the great man on a DuPont-sponsored program, *Cavalcade of America.* I'd been trying to get on radio for months while starving with Virginia. Finally, I got a job. I played Rockefeller in an hour-long weekly program portraying the glories of America. After the show, DuPont complained that I injected political commentary about Rockefeller, and they were right. I had made their wonderful old gentleman seem like Scrooge.

ROGER: Not too long after you were on the radio, I remember being in your home in New York.

ORSON: Where Virginia and I spent only one night, and I was awakened by Hortense who said, "You have diabetes." [Laughter]

ROGER: Exactly. You hosted a dinner party and among the guests was Ethel Merman. I caught a program on television recently featuring her. She was awful.

ORSON: But she was awful for fifty years and everybody loved her. Cole Porter told me he'd rather have her sing a song than anybody in the world.

Orson and his first wife, Virginia, spent many weeks with the Hills in the fall of 1938, flying two days a week to New York for his Campbell Soup broadcasts, and, when at the Hill farm, expanding his high school tour de force *Five Kings* with music by Aaron Copland that was staged by the Theatre Guild and opened on February 27, 1939, at the Colonial Theatre in Boston.

ROGER: No kidding?

ORSON: And I said, "Why? She makes an awful noise when she sings." "But she belts it out. She sells it. You hear every word you've written," he said. [Laughter] Then he added, "All composers agree, we'd rather have Ethel do a show than anybody else because she is capable of turning songs into hits."

ROGER: Did I tell you there was a Todd reunion last month in Woodstock?

ORSON: No.

ROGER: It was quite a gathering with many teary-eyed
           remembrances. My only regret was our time
           together was too short, which prevented me from
           meeting and greeting everyone.

ORSON: I'm certain your performance was masterful.

ROGER: The truth is, I was kind of a selfish schoolman and
           did what I wanted. The faculty ran the school and
           I could be a friend to everyone. As I look back, it
           was a very strange experience, but a good one. I was
           able to share all my enthusiasm with the kids—sailing,
           flying, travel of every kind, literature, and theatre.
           That's why I got by.

ORSON: Got by? You were a triumph. Was the reunion well
           attended?

ROGER: There were well over one hundred and fifty alums.
           We had a banquet and a number of folks got up
           and waxed nostalgic about their Todd days, and
           their unbridled long-ago enthusiasms and dreams.
           Then, we visited what's left of the old campus.

ORSON: Oh, God, how sad.

ROGER: Terribly sad. The Masons bought the school building.
           Each Masonic hall, as I understand it, has an Upper
           Room because the Last Supper was convened in an
           upper room. Our stage has been transformed into
           an upper room.

ORSON: I wouldn't want to see that.

ROGER: I didn't either. It was painful. Thankfully, we didn't
           linger in the Upper Room. During dinner, someone

asked how many former students named a child "Todd." More than twenty named a son after the school. There were a number who had named a child Roger, too. But, for so many to name a child for a school is, I think, very unusual. Can you imagine the alumni of great schools like Groton, Exeter, or Andover doing the same?

ORSON: That really is wonderful. Very touching, particularly since the word means death in German.

ROGER: Yes, with one d. Come to think of it, you're right. [Orson laughs.] Well, we put an extra "d" on it.

ORSON: That means life after death. Is Coach Roskie still in Woodstock?

ROGER: Yes. Roskie is still there.

ORSON: There is no love lost between us.

ROGER: He was in charge of and lived in Grace Hall, the big dormitory that Noble Hill built, the Frank Lloyd Wright prairie style building. Do you remember it?

ORSON: Remember it? You're talking to a man who not only went to Todd, but also lived within those storied stones for most of my time there. There was a running fight between us at all times. Oh, you've forgotten it all. He hated the oriental decorations in my room. He said that they would attract germs.

ROGER: [Laughs.] I do remember how mean he was to you because your unbridled spirit ran him ragged. One night I tried to save you, but I couldn't.

ORSON: I was out on the town. AWOL.

Coach Toney Roskie with two Todd "Red Raider" football players.

ROGER: That's right. I couldn't save you. [Both laugh.] You were crawling in your window and he met you.

ORSON: At the fire escape. [Orson laughs.] A member of the fairer sex more than once prompted my escapes. [Orson laughs.]

ROGER: Similar escapes took place during my childhood at Todd because we didn't have town privileges either.

ORSON: There were no town privileges of any kind when I was there. The one exception was our walking in crocodile to church on Sunday, looking neither to the left nor to the right. And that was it.

ROGER: You stuck to your own little den in Grace Hall all through your years at Todd. You were old enough, and should have gotten the hell out and gone to Johnson's cottage.

ORSON: I didn't want to because of Jim Williams, who was wild and a bore.

ROGER: I remember one thing he did during the performance of *Wings Over Europe* that was kind of clever. The climax occurs when your fellow players are convinced you are a menace, and you're going to—

ORSON: Explode the atomic bomb.

ROGER: You had the atomic bomb, and Williams played a member of parliament who was supposed to shoot you.

ORSON: That's right.

ROGER: His gun didn't go off and he improvised by diving across the table, tossing you to the ground, and damned near killing you.

ORSON: I admire him for that, and I remember him vividly where others have faded away into that ghost land of an uneven memory, but poor Jim Williams. I could pick him out of a crowd of a thousand, and Guggenheim, and Johnny Dexter, and Edgerton Paul, too.

ROGER: Edgerton stayed with you for a while when you went to New York.

ORSON: When he arrived in New York, I got him a job in the theatre where he wasn't bad. Edgy was a serious little fellow with acne, unfortunate in every way, but he cast that all aside when he got into make-up and costume.

ROGER: He was quite short and sensitive about his size.

ORSON: Yes, and I once reminded him that there's never been a great leader of men, on the dictatorial side, who has not been very short. Napoleon, Stalin, name them all, Alexander the Great, Tito, they were all small men. The only exception is Caesar and he wasn't really a dictator. He hardly arrived in Rome when they unsheathed their daggers. He spent most of his career in the Gallic Wars. It's true that all of these real earth-shakers have been extra short. I'll tell you the opposite side of it. Duke Wayne said to me once, "You know, people like us, we've got to be awful careful of them shorties." [Roger laughs.] "Just bear one thing in mind," he said, "When you're in a room with 'em, sit down." [Orson and Roger laugh.]

ROGER: When did he die?

ORSON: About four years ago, the poor guy. After ten years fighting cancer.

ROGER: He must have made some pictures when he was in bad shape.

ORSON: He was operated on successfully and had six or seven more years of active professional life. Then it closed in on him. He was a very sweet man in spite of our differing ideas on politics. In fact, almost all the nice people I've known in the world have been on the right. I think Barry Goldwater was one of the nicest, most charming men. There's no equivalent on the progressive side anymore. That's been true since the death of Roosevelt.

ROGER: Which reminds me of the political columns you wrote in the '40s, and several of which I discovered in my files recently. They're wonderful and timeless. Listening to them brought back memories of us vacationing in the '40s, when you were deep into politics and liberalism. Wherever we went, you were never far from a typewriter writing three columns a week for the *St. Louis Post Dispatch* syndicate. Orson; they're as riveting and relevant today as they were forty years ago. I included them in my file of your early writing, which I brought to help jog your memory when you begin your memoir. The file's on your desk. [Roger walks over to Orson's desk and picks up a large accordion folder and begins rifling through it.] I want to read you a paragraph or two.

ORSON: Oh spare me.

ROGER: [Roger ignores Orson's request.] Let me read a few lines from a piece you titled, *Moral Indebtedness*, a sermon widely printed in the liberal press.

ORSON: Yes, I delivered it in late 1943, at a convention at the Chicago Stadium sponsored by the United Nations Committee to Win the Peace.

ROGER: You delivered it a little more than a year before Hitler fell. I have your original draft, a real Abe Lincoln, back-of-an-envelope penciling on some sheets of hotel stationery. You begin—

ORSON: Don't begin.

ROGER: Humor me; this is more for me than you. [*Center downstage behind a translucent scrim a thirty-year-old Orson delivers the speech.*]

My part in this free meeting is just this: It is to say that to be born free is to be born in debt: to live in freedom without fighting slavery is to profiteer.

By plane last night, I flew over some parts of the republic where American citizenship is a luxury beyond the means of the majority. I rode comfortably in my plane above a sovereign state or two where fellow countrymen of ours can't vote without the privilege of cash. Today I bought my lunch where Negroes may not come except to serve their white brothers and there I overheard a member of some master race or other tell those who listened that something must be done to suppress the Jews....

The scaly dinosaurs of reaction will print it in their newspapers that I am a communist. Communists know otherwise. I am an overpaid movie producer with pleasant reasons to rejoice—and I do—in the wholesome practicability of the profit system. I'm all for making money if it means earning it. Lest, you should imagine that I'm being publicly modest. I'll only admit that everybody deserves at least as many good things as my money buys for me. Surely my right to having more than enough is canceled if I don't use that more to help those who have less. This sense of Humanity's interdependence antedates Karl Marx...

Tonight my subject is the question of Moral Indebtedness. So I'd like to acknowledge here the debt that goes with ownership. I believe, and this has very much to do with my own notion of freedom, I believe I owe the very profit I make to the people I make it from. If this is radicalism, it comes automatically to most of us in show business, it being generally agreed that any public man owes his position to the public. This is a debt payable in service and the highest efforts of the debtor. The extension of this moral argument insists that no man owns anything outright; owning it rent-free.

A wedding never bought a wife. And the devotion of his child for him is no man's for the mere begetting. We must each day earn what we own. A healthy man owes to the sick all that he can do for them. A free man owes to the world's slaves all that he can do for them. And what is to be done is more, much more, than good works, Christmas baskets, bonuses and tips and bread and circuses. There is only one thing to be done with slaves: free them.

When all the fascist armies have formally surrendered, the end of fascism will still be out of sight. This world fight is no melodrama. An armistice is not a happy ending. The people know well that Peace is harder won than War. . . .

No, giving the world back to the inhabitants is too big a job for the merely practical; too brave a task for pessimism. The architects of an enduring peace must be capable of hope. They must believe in people: all the people. They must face the unimaginable vistas of Man's destiny. God grant them steadfast hope, and the rest of us enduring patience. For we must not expect from any leadership a shiny, ready-made millennium in our time. No one of us will live to see a blameless peace. We strive and pray and die for what will be here when we're gone. Our children's children are the ancestors of a free people. We send our greetings ahead of us, to them. To History yet unmade, our greetings. To the generations sleeping in our loins: Be of good heart our children: The fight is worth it.

[Lights dim.]

ORSON: My efforts to support Roosevelt and my political writing prompted some to encourage me to consider a political career beginning in '47 and run for the Senate in either California or Wisconsin.

ROGER: Of course you could have, Orson.

ORSON: No. The times were against me. And you only have
             so much luck of any kind in the world. If I'd been
             born ten years earlier, fifteen years earlier, I would
             have been in a more progressive time, but I was
             really too progressive for the times. There's nobody
             as progressive as I am that's gotten anywhere since
             Roosevelt died. I think I would have had a heart-
             breaking time in Washington.

ROGER: That's, of course, possible.

ORSON: Then, the Kennedys would have come in and
             cut me off at the knees. During a White House
             dinner, when I was campaigning for Roosevelt, in
             a toast, with considerable tongue in cheek, he said,
             "Orson, you and I are the two greatest actors alive
             today." In private that evening, and, on several
             other occasions, he urged me to run for a Senate
             seat either in California or Wisconsin. He wasn't
             alone. There were a number of politician and
             actor friends who took the thought of my running
             seriously, ranging from Alan Cranston to the
             Barrymores. Cranston convinced me that I was
             too liberal to win in California. The Democrats
             in Wisconsin put together some sort of report
             determining my attractiveness to Wisconsin voters.
             They were encouraging. After all, this is the state
             that produced Fighting Bob LaFollette. They
             warned that a certain former circuit court judge,
             Joseph McCarthy, had a big following throughout
             the state, particularly among the powerful dairy
             interests, but I could beat him. Being divorced, I
             convinced myself that there was no hope for a
             divorced candidate to win a senatorial race, or any
             other race for that matter. As Ronnie reminded me
             not long ago, how wrong I was.

ROGER: I remember on one of your trips back to Todd your telling me that John and Ethel Barrymore were encouraging you to run.

ORSON: Yes. The Barrymores, what delightful people. A year or two before she died, Ethel Barrymore asked me about a mutual friend she hadn't seen in years and I told her, "He married a Los Angeles society girl." And she replied, "There is no such thing." "Why not, Miss Barrymore?" I asked, and she answered, "A Los Angeles society girl is anyone who's gone to high school." [Laughter]

ROGER: I was with you and Virginia shortly after you both had had quite a time with Jack, and I remember Virginia was so excited because she finally met him. This was toward the end of his life when he was having so many troubles.

ORSON: That was when we were both in Chicago. You remember when I played *The Green Goddess* in tab at the Palace Theatre?

ROGER: Yes.

ORSON: During several afternoon shows, he joined me on stage playing the high priest.

ROGER: I didn't know that.

ORSON: Yes. It was all in double talk. Hindustani double talk.

ROGER: [Laughter] Drunk or sober, he could be so damned amusing. Remember the story you told me about the sad summer when he was renting a house on the North Shore? His neighbors were entertaining outside and, at about 1:00 in the morning, the host ushered his guests on to the front porch and announced, "This is about the time Barrymore arrives after his performance. Let's sit here and watch the great man make his nightly entrance into his house." John arrives, sees the audience, nods, performs an impromptu buck-and-wing on the sidewalk, stops, and, with a flourish, opens his fly and proceeds to pee as he staggers to the front door. Just before going in, he stops again, gazes at the startled neighbors, and takes a great bow.

ORSON: Oh, God. Tragicomic. I was with him once at the Brown Derby. Did I ever tell you this story?

ROGER: Not that I recall.

ORSON: We were having lunch, and he was regaling me with the horrors of living with and without his fourth, and then current wife, Elaine Barrie. She was giving him a lot of trouble. A few years earlier, in his mid-50s, he married Elaine, a teenager, shortly after she had written him an adoring letter while he was hospitalized in New York. It's not clear if her letter was so beguiling, or that Jack was feeling particularly lonely. Possibly it was a combination of the two. At any rate, he invited her to his hospital room, which led to a white-heat affair that began in the hospital bed. It wasn't long after he bed her that he wed her and found himself in a turbulent and ill-fated marriage. As a nod to the *Tempest*, he referred to her as Ariel and she called him Caliban. Their classic love-hate relationship made for colorful national headlines, four separations, and a lot of pain for Jack. As he began to explain the current marital trauma, he used every four-letter word you ever heard in your life, expressing his predicament, and this was a time, unlike today, when blue language was rarely uttered in public.

We were sitting in one of the booths, and in the next booth was a classic Babbitt and his family from Idaho. As John's fulminations became more volatile and expressive, Babbitt's face became crimson. His apoplexy boiled over and he called the headwaiter. The headwaiter listened for a moment and shrugged his shoulders, which only further outraged the aggrieved party, who then dashed out of the restaurant. Through the front window, I saw him approach a policeman. After a brief animated conversation, the lawman followed Babbitt back into the restaurant. Now, the police-man, the headwaiter, and a couple of bus boys arrived at our table. Jack was in the middle of one of these "cocksucking" this and "mother fucking" that when he espied Babbitt and the others hovering over our table. Without missing a beat, Jack looked up and said, "What is this, peasants with a petition?" [Much laughter]

ROGER: What happened next?

ORSON: Everybody in the restaurant screamed with laughter and there was nothing for the Babbitts to do but leave. As he hustled his family out of this den of iniquity, the outraged father made a little departing speech to the effect that "We've come all the way to visit the glory of Hollywood and we hear this filth. We should have never left home." [Laughter] Jack could be so funny. He wasn't the drunk people thought he was. I discovered that during the last couple of years he was in Hollywood. He told me all about his father, who went mad and was placed in an insane asylum.

ROGER: The ultimate tragic ending.

ORSON: Yes, and Jack was afraid he was going the way

of his father. He used alcohol to hide from that probability. He'd get drunk, or pretend to be drunk, when he really was lost, when he suddenly didn't know how he got where he was or what was happening.

ROGER: It was more forgivable in his mind to pretend he was drunk than admit to himself that, "I'm losing my marbles."

ORSON: Exactly. That's why he took up with the heavy drinkers at the end, his "dear" friends, who sat up every night and murdered him.

ROGER: Wait a minute.

ORSON: Then, when he died, they did that awful thing to him. They took his corpse out of the mortuary for a last night on the town. Gene Fowler, Dave Chasen and Bill Fields, and that painter, that terrible painter, who's dead now, dressed Jack up and took him out for a tour of Hollywood and then put him back in the coffin.

ROGER: They felt he would appreciate the gesture if he were alive, I suppose.

ORSON: He wouldn't have. I was always offended by that final indignity that some people think is riotously funny. Jack was such a kind and generous and funny man and I'm sorry that the favorite stories are about the sad ending because that wasn't the real man.

ROGER: Shakespeare gave Fowler a title for his biography of Jack that softened everything: *Good Night Sweet Prince*. That's so gorgeous that it gives you the feeling that he loved him.

ORSON: They were all extraordinary people, the three
           Barrymore children, and their father. The life of
           their father, Maurice, is one of the most fascinating
           stories in the world. He was a playwright, an actor,
           and a great wit. He was one of the greatest boxers
           of his day and an incredibly beautiful man. He
           adored animals and, when he went touring, he'd
           often pick up more creatures. He'd buy a mountain
           lion here, a weasel there, and then a bear. He
           named his two skunks, Minnehaha and Molly
           Bawn. Eventually, his collection of creatures
           comprised a small zoo that he housed on a farm
           on Staten Island. Maurice was a member of the
           theatrical Lambs Club, in New York, which had a
           house rule banning critics. He once arrived with a
           critic friend of his, and the critic protested, "I
           can't join you. Critics aren't allowed." Maurice
           responded, "Don't worry. Join me. No one has
           ever mistaken you for one." At the end of his
           career, he'd get on the stage and not know one
           word, and had to be led away. He went absolutely
           insane.

ROGER: John had a similar ending, didn't he?

ORSON: Somewhat, but Maurice was younger.

ROGER: Well, that would naturally scare his son.

ORSON: Yes, Maurice was in his early fifties when he first
           suffered a mental collapse. He returned to the stage
           briefly. He went on the road in a melodrama, *The
           Battle of the Strong*, playing the hero. At some
           point in the production, Maurice had a sword fight
           with the villain. One evening, early in the run,
           Barrymore took off the guard from the tip of the
           sword and tried doing in the villain on stage while
           his antagonist was holding a child on his shoulders,

Blanche Sweet, who later became a big silent film
star, and favorite of D.W. Griffith. Shortly there-
after, it fell upon Jack to have his father committed
to the loony bin at Bellevue Hospital. On his first
night in lock-up, he awoke well after midnight;
called out to everyone on the ward that they must
awake and begin acting in a play he had written.
Spotting a sleeping inmate, he bellowed, "Claudius,
King of Denmark, feigns sleep!" The doctors
attending him advised his children that Maurice
was suffering from paresis, a form of dementia that
appears in the late stages of syphilis, and that he
had less than a year to live. On the pretext of taking
him to Philadelphia to audition for a new play, the
children moved him to the Long Island Home at
Amityville. Far from being a snake pit, his final
stop was a comfortable apartment on the grounds
of the sanitarium, an hour's drive from Manhattan.
He made liars out of his doctors. He lived there for
another four years, passing countless hours writing
perfervidly. He told everyone he was writing a new
play, when, in fact, what he scribbled endlessly was
the phrase, "It was a lovely day in June." Years
before, in a saloon, in a moment of reflection, he
penned his own epitaph: "He walked beneath the
stars /And slept beneath the sun; /He lived a life of
going-to-do /And died with nothing done."

ROGER: Why aren't you telling such things on talk shows?

ORSON: I don't want to give my best stuff away.

ROGER: You're so right! And, dammit, now we're back to
my urging you to write your book.

ORSON: When you think of those Barrymores, it's remarkable
that only one of them wanted to be an actor and
that was Ethel.

Roger: Really?

Orson: Lionel spent three years in Paris trying to be a painter and was really quite good. But he decided he was only good and not good enough. Jack spent his youth as a cartoonist for Hearst.

Roger: No.

Orson: Fowler did Jack a great injustice. In his book, he mostly talks about the old days in Hollywood. That's really all you hear.

Roger: I see. "My pal, Jack."

Orson: "My pal Jack" but he knew nothing about the real Jack. He was in Chicago for two and a half years playing in the musical comedy, *The Great Northern*, and God knows what else. This was his introduction to the theatre, after giving up a budding career as a cartoonist and illustrator of theatrical posters and little end-piece cartoons for the Hearst papers. He didn't want to be an actor. His first part on Broadway was playing with his sister in *Captain Jinks of the Horse Marines*. Then, he was a leading man for years until Arthur Hopkins told him he was going to be a great actor. He wasn't very pleased with the thought of a career in the theatre. He reluctantly played Prince Hal. He really didn't want to act.

Roger: What a chapter you've got there and you shouldn't give it away on talk shows.

Orson: Even if I wanted to, they don't let you tell anything fully enough. I could do a great television special on the Barrymores, the whole family, including the old lady, Mrs. Drew, John Drew, and all of them.

There are so many Barrymores. It's an extraordinary story. Barrymore is a fake name, a stage name. Their name is Blythe.

ROGER: Really?

ORSON: Yes, because Maurice Barrymore was an aristocrat. He was an English gentleman, the youngest son of a Lord. In order to hide his low profession as an actor, he took a stage name, Barrymore. They all took it. But it's not their legal name. They're all Blythes.

ROGER: Who is Drew?

ORSON: Drew is old Mrs. Drew, Louisa Lane Drew. She's on the other side of the family. Her third marriage to John Drew, who was also an actor, produced three offspring. Her third child, Georgiana, married Maurice. In the 1850s, her husband, John, ran the Arch Street Theatre in Philadelphia. He proved to be a poor manager. His wife, Louisa, took charge. For three decades, she ran the place with great panache and built it into one of the stellar repertory companies in all of American theatre. She was a remarkably versatile and talented actress, best known for Mrs. Malaprop. She was also quite an accomplished Shakespearean actor, playing many female roles and not a few "breeches" parts. Her Mark Antony and Romeo were particularly memorable. After she closed the Arch Street Theatre, she toured with her great friend, Joseph Jefferson, in his production of *The Rivals*, and God knows what else. She was the greatest actress-manager in America before the days of Fannie Kimble, and she could remember Keane, and all that. Yes, John comes from a long line of actors on his mother's side.

ROGER: God, what a story.

ORSON: Jack, like his father, was a great animal lover. He
           had a kennel full of Great Danes. He told me with
           a straight face that while listening to *War of the
           Worlds,* he sprang to the kennel, opened the pens,
           and bellowed to the beasts, "Fend for yourselves."
           I've told you of taking Jack to the opening of
           Kane?

ROGER: No, you took him?

ORSON: Yes, the opening of *Citizen Kane* in Los Angeles, at
           the El Capitan Theatre. I went with Dolores del
           Rio, John Barrymore, King Vidor, and King
           Vidor's wife. Our party arrived after a dinner at
           King Vidor's, in a limousine, with searchlights
           twirling. "And here comes Norma Shearer's car,"
           and all that. "And here comes John Barrymore,"
           an announcer intoned. "And with him is Orson
           Welles whose picture you are about to see. What
           have you got to say, Mr. Barrymore?" We're on
           320 stations and Jack dramatically announces,
           "Now it can be told, Orson is, in fact, the bastard
           son of Ethel and the Pope." [Much laughter] At
           which point, we're off the air on all 320 stations
           with organ music playing. "Ethel and the Pope."
           [Laughing]

ROGER: "Ethel and the Pope."

ORSON: That was his contribution.

ROGER: He was brilliant in his old age.

ORSON: Oh, he was absolutely brilliant.

ROGER: Who was the bedridden fellow who had worked

At the start of filming *Citizen Kane*, Orson changed the name of Kane's political rival in the race for Governor of New York from Edward Rogers to Jim Gettys, acknowledging Hortense's lawyer father, Arthur Lincoln "Granddad" Gettys, who was "Big Jim's" polar opposite, and in frail health. He died in March 1941, two months before the film was released.

with MacArthur and was a good friend of the Barrymores?

ORSON: Ned Sheldon. He had written *Nigger* and *Romance*, famous plays in the late teens and early twenties. Then he was stricken with a rare type of arthritis, which paralyzed and blinded him. He remained in a dark room only able to speak, and he more or less ran the New York theatre for thirty years. None of us did anything without talking to him. He called me after every broadcast and told me what he liked and what he didn't like. The Lunts and Helen Hayes, everybody went to him. He was sort of an Oracle. Ned was responsible for sending me to Chicago to attend the death of Jack Barrymore. Ned called me and said Jack was dying in Chicago. That's why I arrived in Chicago and found Lionel and Ethel who had also been sent by Ned. They hadn't seen each other in years. We couldn't find

Jack at the Hotel Ambassador East, where he was living, and we got in a car and drove around town. Finally, it occurred to me that he must be in some cathouse. So, we got the addresses of the best ones—

ROGER: Now wait a minute. You started talking about Barrymore's funeral—

ORSON: I didn't talk about the funeral.

ROGER: And now you're talking about his last days.

ORSON: I'm talking about Jack's dying.

ROGER: Oh, his dying?

ORSON: It's not a funeral. Dying sometimes takes forty years. John lived four years after that. But, Ned, thinking John was dying, sent me to Chicago, as well as Lionel and Ethel, and here was this great man pie-eyed in a cathouse. The three great Barrymores, who hadn't seen each other since *Rasputin*, were reunited in a bordello and there followed a great warm weekend. It was a fascinating time, and Jack returned the following Monday night to that terrible play, *My Dear Children*, where he played an over-emoting Shakespearean actor, past his prime, and debt-ridden. It was a painful self-parody, but he still was holding his head up, trying to pay his debts. That's why he did those things toward the end. I can't even laugh at it, because I know the real tragedy. It was just awful. He was profoundly sick. What lasts in the common memory are all the funny stories that were told about his peeing. He worked as a man of honor because he owed debts. He could have quit and been sick and let Solomon take care of him, but he didn't. That's why I have such admiration and affection for him.

ROGER: He was trying to pay back some of his debts.

ORSON: He did, he did. He paid a lot back. He did all those terrible movies at the end, and that play, not to make a fool of himself, which he knew he was doing, but to pay back. We had some great times after Chicago. During his decline, he went on the radio for three years with Rudy Vallee and I was on almost every show. During this period, there were times when he was very aggressive, funny, and in pretty good shape.

ROGER: I'd forgotten that. I should re-read Fowler.

ORSON: Don't read *Good Night, Sweet Prince*. It's a lie, presenting only Jack's worst side. It's a narrative of drunken people, delightfully described, but they weren't delightful, they were just disgusting and tragic and they were all at the end of the road, or close to it, sitting around trying to be accepted. I hated how they used Jack, were entertained by him, but never really tried to understand or help him. I never wanted to be or was a part of that crowd, though I was very fond of Ralph Fields, who was a part of that little gang. They all encouraged Jack and he drank more because of it. But he did not die of alcohol, that's all wrong. He was never an alcoholic. He drank a lot and most of it was to cover the fact that he thought he was going mad.

ROGER: Jack certainly deserves some space in your book.

ORSON: Oh, I'm going to do a lot about him and the whole family. Look at Lionel and the drugs. It started because of a virulent case of arthritis, which reduced him to living in a wheelchair. One of those Goddamn Beverly Hills doctors got him hooked on hard stuff. He was hooked for twelve years, and, one day, he decided to quit. He went to his home, called the studio, and said that he wouldn't be free for a month. He locked himself in his house and cured himself cold turkey. Now, that's something. He was then sixty-nine, my age, when he did it. That takes strength of character.

ROGER: Well, that didn't get him out of the wheelchair, just—

ORSON: What do you want? It didn't make him fly through the air either. I also got to know Ethel well the last two or three years of her life. I became tremendously fond of her, too. They were all unbelievably crafty people. Now there's a new Barrymore star, Drew, an eight-year-old, who's the granddaughter of Jack, and she's wonderful.

ROGER: Did Jack die of cirrhosis of the liver from too much booze?

ORSON: The cause of death was listed as cirrhosis of the liver and pneumonia. But, what I think really got him was the same disease that afflicted poor Rita, Alzheimer's.

ROGER: That's right. They didn't have a name for it then.

ORSON: Yes. Poor Rita, I was so shocked by her blackouts.

ROGER: Oh, God.

ORSON: Becky [Rebecca Welles, Orson and Rita's daughter] goes to see Rita next week.

ROGER: Oh, really?

ORSON: Yes. She hasn't seen her in seven years.

ROGER: She won't recognize her daughter.

ORSON: No. Rita now doesn't even know Yasmin [Rita's daughter Yasmin Khan], whom she sees every day. I'm awfully worried about Becky's visit. I wish I could discourage her because she hasn't seen Rita in so many years. It's going to be a very shocking experience. Becky's a sensitive girl.

ROGER: It would scare anybody, "This is my mother that's no longer my mother."

ORSON: Rita barely knows me now. I smile sweetly, but no recognition. I saw Rita three years ago at a function the Reagans threw for Sinatra. When it was over, I came over to her table and I saw that she was very beautiful, very reposed looking, and didn't know me at first. After about four minutes of speaking, I could see that she realized who I was and she began to cry quietly.

ROGER: You were probably wiser than Hortense and I. We saw Rita in Paris in the '60s, and thought her problem was alcoholism.

ORSON: It wasn't. She abused herself with alcohol, but that isn't what did it at all. It didn't take many drinks to trigger her trauma. She'd have one or two martinis and she was off. I never thought she was an alcoholic. I knew that she was psychotic. It certainly imitated alcoholism in every superficial way. I'll tell you why I always thought it wasn't alcoholism. Having had a drunken father, a drunken aunt, and drunken friends, having observed alcoholism all my life, I've noticed that people's personalities change when they get very drunk. They get happier or they get meaner or something. You know what I mean?

ROGER: Yes.

ORSON: There's no drunk I've ever known who was the same man or woman when drunk. They become somebody else. Rita never changed at all. Nothing happened that showed a side of her that you didn't see when she was sober, and that convinced me that her troubles were physical or psychological. God knows she was in pain when we were married. She used to fly into these rages, never at me, never once, always at Harry Cohen or her father or her mother or her brother. She would break all the furniture and she'd get in a car and I'd have to get in the car and try to control her. She'd drive up in the hills suicidally. Terrible, terrible nights. And I just saw this lovely girl destroying herself. I admire Yasmin so much.

ROGER: She must be quite a kid to be so devoted to her mother.

ORSON: She is.

ROGER: The last time I saw her she was about twelve years old. Rita was quite rational and I have movies of Yasmin and Becky swimming together.

ORSON: Yasmin was always a delightful kid with a sunny, positive personality. She's very bright. Her grandfather was one of the smartest men I ever met, the Aga Khan III, who, among his other accomplishments, was the Chairman of the League of Nations for three years in the '30s.

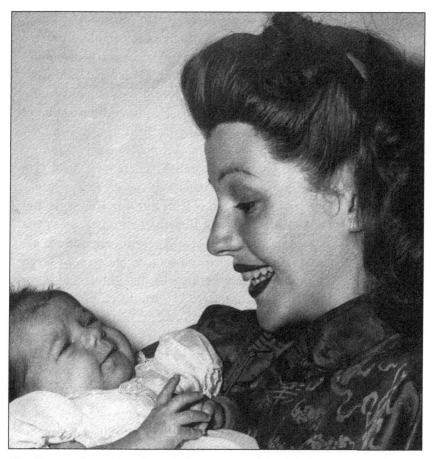

Rita Hayworth and daughter, Rebecca, on a visit with Orson to Todd in early 1945.

ROGER: What was his lifestyle?

ORSON: His lifestyle? Well, you remember that—

ROGER: I don't remember anything.

ORSON: In 1931, the Ismailis celebrated Sir Sultan's 50th anniversary as Aga Khan III by sending him his weight in gold. Twenty-five years later, they sent the portly gentleman his weight in diamonds.

ROGER: Oh, that's right. [Laughter]

ORSON: I don't have to go on after that. Suffice it to say, his lifestyle was exceedingly comfortable. I don't think he could have been what he was without being very rich. He was a religious head, and his grandson, Aga Khan IV, is still the religious head, like the Pope, of a sect of Hindus. Almost none of them live in India, many of them now live in South America. Of course, they're hardly Hindu because Aly was half-Italian. There have been many infusions of European blood, so they're not very Eastern. The fourth wife of old Aga Khan, Begum Aga Khan III, Yvette Blanche Labrousse, was Miss France in 1930, and is still very much around, a great figure in European society. She's about seven feet tall, a former manicurist, [laughter] and is enormously impressive as a royal figure, and very bright. Of course, her husband married so many times and had so many mistresses due to a raging case of coitolimia. Am I pronouncing it correctly?

ROGER: I don't even know what it is?

ORSON: The desire to fuck every fifteen minutes. He passed the condition on to his son. Aly once observed, "Except for Rita, it's hard keeping track of all my other wives and lovers. They were just whoever happened to be handy." [Laughter] He was very charming. I first knew him when I was eight years old and he was twelve.

ROGER: No kidding?

ORSON: Yes. I was sent to a place in New York, made famous in the late '60s, Woodstock.

ROGER: Where the big rock concert took place, the hippie gathering.

ORSON: Somebody had a big house where I was sent after my mother died, and nearby were all the children of the Aga Khan. I played with them and we've known each other all our lives. The children must have been staying with a friend of their Italian mother's, and this friend must have been a friend of my mother. She wouldn't have been a friend of my father. I can't imagine it. The Watsons had an art colony nearby and I would go and visit them every week, and I remember that vividly because Emily Watson introduced me to the mysteries of playing doctor. [Laughter]

ROGER: How old was this junior minx?

ORSON: A little older than I, a blooming ten or something. Anyway, girls are born grown up. But, she was full of what I later discovered to be misinformation. [Laughing]

ROGER: But maybe this tryst had something to do indirectly with your ending up at Todd.

ORSON: No, no, that was another prompting. I was an innocent young boy who was always being led astray by women. This was a hectic period when Dadda and my father shared an apartment in Chicago. I went for about six weeks to a public school in Chicago, which I hated, and I persistently pretended to be sick. One afternoon, upon returning from school, I put the thermometer on the hot water bottle, which moved Dadda to send me to the hospital where they took out my appendix.

ROGER: [Laughs]

ORSON: I kept saying, "Wait a minute, I'm feeling better." [Laughter] Nobody would listen. That episode

ended my brief excursion into public education
and prompted my coming to Todd.

ROGER: How did you end up in Madison?

ORSON: That was before. Madison was shortly after
my mother's death in 1924. I attended the last
few weeks of a camp called Indianola, run by
Dr. Frederick Mueller, who was the head of the
University of Wisconsin's Psychology department.
One ill-fated afternoon, the good doctor invited
me to his home, and it turned out he had
designs on me. I no sooner entered his home than
he began chasing me about the place. I escaped
with my virginity at some peril to my life by
climbing out a window, running to the Madison
railway station, and returning to Chicago. You
never heard all of this?

ROGER: I knew this Mueller was running a camp, but I
didn't know anything untoward took place...

ORSON: Yes, he ran it as a racket. I returned to Chicago,
where Dadda, not my father, met me because my
father had gone off to Trinidad. I began living with
Dadda and that's when I began my brief incarceration
in a public school and where I met captivating
little Miss Levy, who organized a small club for
orgiastic practices in the basement of her apartment
building. One day, Mrs. Levy appeared in our
apartment denouncing Dadda for allowing me to
become a raving sex monster who had deflowered
her daughter and I remember her ranting, "Look
what happened to that little boy Bobby Franks at
the hands of Leopold and Loeb." I remember that
very clearly. There was supposed to be a strong
connection between the Leopold and Loeb murder
and what we were playing down in the basement.

Have I lost you? It was just one sexual encounter after another. It didn't calm down until I got to Woodstock [Laughter] and was able to catch my breath. I really had a terrible feeling. I didn't know what Leopold and Loeb had done. I'd seen the headlines, and I suddenly realized that these innocent foolings around that we were doing in the basement would send you to the death house. So that's why I went rather meekly to this reform school, which was the Todd School for Boys. The first time I saw you, you were walking up a snowy sidewalk, in the late fall, just before Halloween, with your open galoshes flopping and rather too much hair for those days, looking artistic and rather brigandish. It was then that I declared to myself that I would make that man my friend no matter what the price. And the price was beginning my career on the stage performing in your musical comedy, *Finesse the Queen*, and singing, "Ah Gondolivia, Gondolivia, land of melody."

ROGER: [Laughs]

ORSON: I thought that those flopping galoshes were the most dramatic thing I'd ever seen. In addition to performing a bit of magic, I cobbled together a Tennyson comic act, which included some snappy material, with the ending line, "Do you see those gracious meadows?" "No, but I see the Noble Hills," which absolutely brought the house down. [Laughter] All my early acting and magic efforts were to impress you and try to save me from the horrors of mandatory gymnastics and the prospect of falling into the fabled safety net. I was living in dread of that gymnastic net of yours. I kept asking myself what I must do to have you spend more of your time on the stage and less time on the gym floor.

ROGER: Before your arrival, madcap musicals were frequent fare. I remember you were in one of them I had written.

ORSON: I was in two of your musicals. In *Around the World*, I played a leading role. In *Finesse the Queen*, I was one of the chorus girls.

ROGER: I thought you always were a lead. I don't think you were in the chorus. Your legs were too chubby to be a convincing chorus girl, but, more to the point, you were too damn good to simply be a member of the anonymous chorus.

ORSON: I remember we played *Finesse the Queen* in Rockford, shades of where you are now. The worst quarrel I ever had with Hortense was in Rockford, backstage before the performance, on the subject of make-up. [Laughter] I thought I knew better. Hort was convinced she knew better, and admonished me to, "Just be still and let me do the makeup." I'm convinced my fascination, if not obsession, with the art of make-up is an effort to, in some small measure, gain Hort's approval.

ROGER: Horty's approval of you never faltered from the moment she laid her eyes on you until the day she died. The recent Todd alumnae gathering was the first time I greeted the alums without Horty. Her wit and laughter were greatly missed everyone told me, but no one knows that better than I.

ORSON: And I.

ROGER: Do you remember the charming, if florid, prose you wrote for our Todd Theatre Festival mailing piece? I ran across a copy the other day. Where is it, oh, here it is. If you'll indulge me, it starts

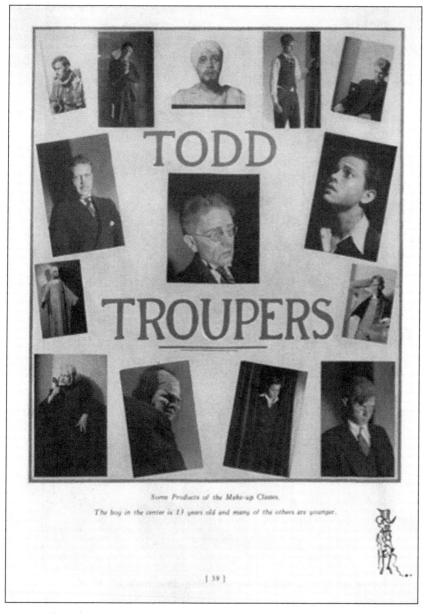

A page from *Todd: A Community Devoted to Boys and Their Interests.*

out, *Like a wax flower under a bell of glass, in the paisley and gingham county of McHenry is Woodstock, grand capital of mid-Victorianism in the Midwest. Towering over a Square full of Civil War*

Hortense Gettys Hill on her wedding day, June 10, 1916.

monuments, a bandstand and a springhouse is the edifice in the picture. This very rustic and rusticated thing is a municipal office building, a public library, and fire department and what is more to our purpose, an honest-to-horsehair Opera House. Not everyone was pleased with your characterization of the town.

Many of the city fathers were mad at you and me for what they considered our making fun of the town with your effusive—

ORSON: Well, there was nothing to make fun of. What I wrote was in affection and admiration.

ROGER: Of course it was. Now the town burghers quote your passage of praise in all their promotional pieces. Times have changed and the town now treasures its roots, which you extolled. But, fifty years ago, Woodstock was the home of the Woodstock Typewriter factory, the Oliver Typewriter Company, and several other large and prosperous manufacturing operations. The city fathers of that era wanted to be the new Elgin, a prosperous manufacturing center, home of the Elgin Watch Company, and twenty miles south of Woodstock. They didn't share your bucolic, sepia-colored image of the town. They didn't want your charm at all. "Watch Woodstock grow!" was their ceaseless mantra.

ORSON: [Laughs heartily]

ROGER: A photograph that Johnny Dexter sent me [laughing] is completely confusing. I think it's one of those blackouts we used to do for Saturday night entertainment. You are in a tux, and draped over your tux is a long checkered coat. You're in front of a microphone holding a reading glass and staring intently at another boy, dressed as a young Sherlock Holmes. I plan to include this photo in the revised *Time and Chance*.

ORSON: I begin to dread the second edition of your autobiography.

ROGER: Oh, you mean what I'll add to my Welles chapter?

ORSON: Yes.

ROGER: Oh, Orson.

ORSON: I just don't like myself characterized as a tall tale
              spinner, a teller of stories that aren't to be believed,
              because I'm going to publish a book in a year
              or two, and I want people to believe what I tell
              them.

ROGER: They will. Nothing I say will detract or contradict
              you. Yours is going to be the greatest memoir that's
              ever been written and I know it's going to end all
              your financial problems.

ORSON: No. No. All you can make is a million dollars on it
              and I'll have to do three of them just to meet my
              obligations.

ROGER: Can you get rid of some of your overhead?

ORSON: I can't get rid of my obligations. You've been more
              clever financially over the years than I. You attracted
              the pigeons effortlessly, with much more guile than
              I've ever managed. I have a lot of things that I can
              sell, but it costs money to get them in a position
              to sell. A cutter gets a thousand a week, where he
              used to get a hundred and fifty. These are the kinds
              of things that make it tough. I would love to have
              it all wiped away except for *Lear, The Other Side
              of the Wind*, and if they aren't possible, I wish to
              God they'd tell me now so I don't go on living in
              a chimera. I'm so superstitiously afraid that they
              won't happen that, at times, I wish it could all be
              wiped away and then some nice university would
              put me on one of those things they do with elderly,

dignified figures from the past, and let me get on with my book.

ROGER: Yes, your book and get some lectures and things on tape.

ORSON: Lectures are a headache. I could make a fortune on lectures, but they are so fatiguing. The way they book you, you're in San Francisco on Tuesday, Scranton on Wednesday, and Denver on Thursday. Then you have to take a hop to Fort Worth on Friday, and from there to Seattle on Saturday. You're going back and forth across the country by plane, sitting in airports endlessly. They tell me that I'd get fifteen thousand a lecture, which is up there in the Kissinger range, but you have to commit for a year in the future that on the 16th of September next year you will be in Waukesha. As long as I have a hope of a movie, I don't dare make such commitments.

ROGER: I just want your lectures transcribed to tapes, Goddamn it. I'm convinced that there would be a sizeable market for your readings and ruminations.

ORSON: Yes, after *Lear* and *The Other Side of the Wind*, while working on my book, I want to develop a series of talks, like Dickens, and take them on the road as well as put them on tape.

ROGER: Oh, I think that is so important.

ORSON: The trouble, I fear, is that few people under the age of forty will recognize the people I'm going to talk about. So, a glossary ought to be published, like those for Shakespeare, telling you what a bodkin means. You can't suddenly talk about John Drew. Who the hell was he? Nor do they know who John Barrymore was. It's sad commentary, because all the best stories are the old ones, and there's a limit to how many fascinating and insightful anecdotes I can throw out about one or the other current superstars now because A, they'd sue me and B, all the stories revolve around snorting cocaine. I'm tempted to include a great story that my father used to tell about the disappearance of one of my great aunts. Of course, I never took it seriously. She was riding in a double rickshaw that had two coolies pulling it and two passengers sitting together. About the time of their disappearance, there was a lot of unpleasantness and unrest in the country. According to this story, my great aunt and grandmother, who survived, arrived in a melee of angry Chinese and the coolies let go of the traces and they fell over backwards into the crowd. One of the aunts was never seen again. [Laughter.] "Well, there went aunt whomever-it-was into white slavery." We'll never know. But that was a perfectly serious family story. There was another family story about Aunt Dot who had gone down the main street of Johnstown during the great flood on a grand piano. That was her distinction. Well, I never believed that as a child. When I told it to people, it was good for a laugh. Nobody believed it. I got a letter this year from an old, old lady who had been in the Johnstown flood and she had heard me tell this story on a talk show and she said, "I saw your aunt." [Uproarious laughter.] I never knew anything more about it except that one sentence, "Aunt Dot went down the main street of the town on a grand piano."

ROGER: Your idea of a glossary makes a lot of sense.

ORSON: Yes, because when you start to talk about the great Russian basso, Feodor Chaliapin, for instance, who

the hell knows who he is? There isn't one person, I
suppose, in a million, who knows that I was ever in
the theatre.

ROGER: Your talks would lead them to read something
about Chaliapin, and it's a very interesting
combination. I never thought of it before, a
lecture with a glossary.

ORSON: I've always suspected that Chaliapin was my father
because he had a big love affair with my mother at
the time when it would have counted. And I had a
very strange experience when I went to Rome after
the war and met some of the family, including his
daughter, who is easily the most beautiful girl you
ever saw in your life. And I thought, "Can that
possibly be my sister?" Then I looked at pictures of
the old man and me. He looks a lot more like I do
than my father. My father was a small-boned man,
entirely different than me, and Chaliapin was
exactly like I am. I've always believed that secretly.
I once experienced a truly melodramatic scene
when I was in a dressing room in London getting
ready for a performance in the afternoon. The
dresser said, "There's a young lady to see you." I
said, "Tell her I can only give her a minute because
I'm getting ready for a show." She was strikingly
turned out, an American with a Bennington
Finishing School accent. I said, "Hello." She said,
"I just wanted to look at you." I said, "Well,
alright, now you've seen me." She said, "Of
course, you know who I am, and I know who
your father was." I said, "I really don't." And she
responded, "Then, I won't stir anything up," and
she left.

ROGER: Really?

ORSON: Yes.

ROGER: Was she about your age?

ORSON: Not my age. I would say a little bit older, but not
            much, a couple of years. Very attractive.

ROGER: Fascinating. But she didn't go any further? She
            just—

ORSON: She wouldn't go any further. When she realized
            that I didn't know her story, she wasn't going to
            tell it to me. She might have been another off-
            spring of Chaliapin. He could have left them all
            over the world.

ROGER: [Laughing] Yes.

ORSON: He was an old Russian peasant with a sexual vitality
            that I would give my life to have. [Laughter] He
            used to hold me on his lap and when I prayed to
            God as a little child, I always prayed to the image
            in my mind of Chaliapin dressed for Boris
            Godunov. I remember him saying one day, "What
            do you want to be when you grow up?" I said, "Of
            course I want to be a great basso, like you."
            Decades later, I lost my voice before a play. I went
            to a French specialist for six weeks of daily therapy
            and he said to me, "You know what's wrong with
            your voice?" I said, "No." He responded, "You
            were born to be a heldentenor," a heroic tenor in
            Wagner, that kind of thing. And he added, "You
            forced your voice into a basso, baritone-basso for
            some reason when you were young." Of course,
            that was in Dublin.

ROGER: Humm.

Feodor Chaliapin as Boris Godunov, 1915.

ORSON: One wonders if it's true or not. At Todd, I don't
          recall trying to force it down. Though, perhaps, I
          was trying to be Chaliapin? Who knows?

ROGER: Who indeed? This project sounds promising.

ORSON: Oh, Roger, what a joy to be again in your presence. Were I forty, or even years younger, I would insist this not end at least before we heard the chimes at midnight. But, I'm feeling infinitely old and ready to adjourn for the evening.

ROGER: It's past eleven, and way past my bedtime. It's approaching two in the morning on my internal clock. "*O sleep, O gentle sleep, Nature's soft nurse*" will have no trouble weighing my eyelids down tonight.

ORSON: Then what does Henry say? "*Oh God! That one might read the book of fate, /And see the revolution of the times /Make mountains level, and the continent, Weary of solid firmness, melt itself /Into the sea!*" We'll read more from the book of fate and look closer at the revolution of the times tomorrow. [They both rise out of their chairs.] Good night.

ROGER: Good night. [They embrace, disengage, and slowly head to their respective bedrooms, Orson departs stage right, and Roger leaves stage left.]

[Lights dim.]

Hortense Hill and Rita Hayworth enjoying one another's company in an actual funhouse during a break in the filming of *The Lady from Shanghai.*

Orson, Rita Hayworth, Hortense, and Roger Hill, onboard the *S.S. Catalina*, 1947.

ACT ONE
SCENE SEVEN
SEPTEMBER 17, 1983
BY NOW I SHOULD BE INURED TO A LIFETIME
OF SETBACKS, BUT, I'M NOT

Welles-Hill libraries, Orson's telephone rings.

ORSON: Hello.

ROGER: Orson. This is Roger.

ORSON: How are you?

ROGER: I'm fine. Have you tried to call me recently?

ORSON: Yes, repeatedly since I returned from London and without any luck. That's why I sent you a telegram begging for your new number.

ROGER: I received it today. [Laughs.] Yes, I have a new number and new device to record my callers. I was calling to give it to you. You're back from London. Did you complete your work in *Where Is Parsifal?* Have you had any success in your ongoing battle with Khomeini's people and the French for the negative to *The Other Side of the Wind?*

ORSON: Yes, to your first question, and not much to your second. *Parsifal's* pretty thin going. It was just a quick job I took because I'm hoping the fellow who is backing this film, Alexander Salkind, will invest in *Lear*. He's shown interest in backing me and he wanted me in *Parsifal.* What I won't do to

finance my films. He and his father produced
The Trial. I'm hoping he will do the same for *Lear.*
The Khomeini government has given up its rights,
but the Shah's brother-in-law insists he has the
rights. The French court thought otherwise and
declared it was mine, but, because the negative is
in France, the court ruled crazily that it's a French
film. The French court ruled that the decision as
to whether or not I could take the film out of the
country would be the purview of an arbitrator.
The arbitrator continues to stall, and I just couldn't
afford to keep waiting. Sitting week after week
in my hotel, waiting for a positive word, and
receiving none, turned my thoughts to bowing
out of the movie business and looking for more
fruitful gardens to attend. But, here I am back in
Los Angeles resolved to continue fighting the
good fight to finish the films that need to be
finished and begin *Lear.* Now, Salkind is avoiding
me, just like I thought you're trying to do.

ROGER: More damned delays.

ORSON: By now I should be inured to a lifetime of
setbacks, but, I'm not. When I called your old
number, I was greeted by the steely tone of the
operator's voice informing me that the number
has been changed.

ROGER: [Still laughing.] That's right. I'm a big shot, and I
don't want to be reached. Have you ever had to
change your number because somebody—

ORSON: Yes. I have a real problem because some people
that I want to be able to reach me are unable to
do so, and those I'd rather not have contact me
somehow find my number. I don't know how to
sort them out.

ROGER: Well, we're back in communication.

ORSON: The late season Midwest tornados that have been making the news are quite unusual. I noted with alarm that a few touched down in Northern Illinois. None in Rockford, I trust. God still loves you.

ROGER: Yes. We're lucky. We did have winds that exceeded eighty miles an hour. A lot of people working in the new Sears Tower in Chicago were scared and evacuated the building. The building literally wiggled, which would be enough to unnerve anyone. A few days ago, we received a warning that we were in a tornado danger zone, and were advised that if you find yourself in a car when a tornado touches down, you're to find a culvert and crawl into it.

ORSON: Dear God. How are you going to find a culvert at such a moment of crisis? That's a little like Mr. Reagan's fellow telling us to dig a six-foot hole. I'm told there's a book on the subject if you can believe it.

ROGER: Yes, I've read it, *With Enough Shovels: Reagan, Bush, and Nuclear War*. The author posits that to protect yourself against nuclear fallout, you simply dig a hole, get inside, close the hatch, and make sure there's a foot of soil between you and Armageddon. You Californians not only have to worry about the bomb, but also the San Andreas Fault.

ORSON: Oh, yes. People are always talking about the old buildings that will fall down, but I keep looking at these new forty-story glass boxes, which give me pause. There was a mild earthquake in an outlying town about three years ago and the only building that was totally destroyed was one of those new glass boxes. It was built according to all the earthquake-proof specifications, but down it crumbled.

ROGER: Do you remember an earthquake-proof hotel in Japan that Frank Lloyd Wright designed?

ORSON: Yes, of course. You know, they destroyed his lovely Imperial Hotel. That was Japan's gratitude for Wright's masterpiece. This great triumph, built in 1922, stood when everything else fell down during the Kanto earthquake in 1923. It was torn down in 1968 to make way for a bigger hotel. It wasn't considered a cultural monument at all. There was an outcry in every other country, but not in Japan. It was beautiful, typically Wright, with long, horizontal lines. So much for his triumph. [Sadly laughs.] So much for a reverence for the past.

ROGER: So much of Chicago's architectural past has been obliterated.

ORSON: Chicago was the home of the great American architects, Wright, of course, his mentor, Louis Sullivan, the so-called "prophet of modern architecture," Daniel Burnham, and Mies van der Rohe. Carson Pirie was supposed to be the most beautiful building of its time. Does it still stand?

ROGER: It's there, but they tore down one of Sullivan's great triumphs, the Chicago Stock Exchange. I don't know if it's culturally important, but the once glorious Chicago Theatre on State Street is in danger of being taken down by a wrecking ball. Do you remember it?

ORSON: It was famous. That's where Paul Ash and his orchestra used to play.

ROGER: It's not as renowned as Radio City in New York. There was the great Wurlitzer in the Chicago Theatre.

ORSON: Oh, yes, it was mighty. I remember it well and
              they're trying to tear it down? Well, of course,
              nobody goes to movies in aesthetically pleasing
              theatres anymore. They go, instead, to theatres that
              have been transformed into little viewing boxes.
              Have you seen them?

ROGER: Of course, where four to six theatres are clustered
              together in one building.

ORSON: The ratio of the screen to the audience is equivalent
              to the television in your home. The heart of
              America is the shopping mall, and these multi-
              screens are jammed together there. I think people
              make mistakes and go into the wrong ones, seeing
              an "adult" movie when they thought they were
              going to see the latest Disney offering. Isn't it terrible
              that the word "adult," like "gay" has been totally
              ruined?

ROGER: Yes, but I think it's maybe just as well that our
              children learned the truth about sex earlier than
              we did.

ORSON: Of course, if they had the benefit of Maurice
              Bernstein's lectures on sex, they'd have had nothing
              to fear.

ROGER: The poor guy would become so embarrassed
              whenever the subject was broached.

ORSON: One of his early lessons involved drawing a circle
              on the blackboard and that was the end of the
              evening [Roger and Orson laugh.]

ROGER: I don't think I ever told you this. Noble Hill hid a
              lot of student contraband in a deep closet that was
              under the grand staircase leading to his apartment

Back parlor of Wallingford Hall, 1926. The "deep closet" door is to the left of the French door.

in Wallingford Hall. He thought his son wouldn't discover this hiding place. There was a book on the mysterious subject of Eros in that closet. It was illustrated and as explicit as any contemporary book on the subject. It was written entirely in a throat-clucking tone. It told about the delights of harems, and so forth, and asked its readers, "Wasn't this awful?" I'll bet you that I was one of the few seven-year-old kids at the turn of the century who knew the meaning of fellatio and cunnilingus. It was a sexual encyclopedia [they both laugh]. Besides that, Noble hid a large tin carton containing hundreds of cigarettes that he'd taken from boys who had strayed from the path of rectitude. Instead of throwing them away, he stored them in the closet. It was in that dark forbidden enclosure that I tasted my first tobacco.

Roger Edward "Skipper" Hill sporting his first sailor suit at age four.

ORSON: You had a double education in that treasure-trove.

ROGER: That's right.

ORSON: I'll be calling you at your new number.

ROGER: I hope, when you call, it will be to tell me that
           Salkind is financing *Lear.*

ORSON: I've spent too much of my life waiting unprofitably for calls from potential backers. I'm no longer allowing myself to become giddy at the prospect of tomorrow's expectations. But, instead, guardedly optimistic.

ROGER: Stay optimistic. Good-bye.

[Lights dim.]

CURTAIN

The October 9, 1929 wedding party of Orson's guardian, Dr. Maurice Bernstein, his bride, Edith Mason, a leading soprano of the Chicago Opera Association, in front of Wallingford Hall; ebullient fourteen-year-old Orson to their right; to their left are Hortense and Roger Hill.

ACT TWO
SCENE ONE

JUNE 21, 1984
I'M REMEMBERING IT THE WAY IT
OUGHT TO HAVE BEEN

Interior of Orson and Roger's libraries. Roger's telephone rings.

ROGER: Hello.

ORSON: Roger, how are you?

ROGER: Fine except I'm just having a bit of trouble getting to sleep.

ORSON: What are you doing to solve your problem?

ROGER: Television therapy. I've developed a strange habit. I find that I can go to sleep eventually if I have a little noise in my bedroom. There's a constant news program I use as a soporific.

ORSON: I know what I have to get you. I've seen it advertised and I've been tempted to get it for myself.

ROGER: Oh, I know what you're going to say and it's no good.

ORSON: The sound of the sea and the wind and the rain. It's no good, huh?

ROGER: It doesn't work for me very well. [Laughter] Which reminds me of a passage in a poem by Virginia's poet-uncle, J.U. Nicolson, "Let others sing songs of the joys of the byways, /The trysts in the gloaming, the lays of the lark, /Let others delight in the throngs on the highways, /The bustle and babble from dawn unto dark. /The droning of bees and the murmur of crowds /Are drowned in the hymn of the hum of the shrouds, /And it's ho! for a ship to go booming down my ways, /A sloop or a schooner, a brig or a bark."

ORSON: I heard you pull it off more than once.

ROGER: The truth is, as a sailor, the sound of humming shrouds is not a terribly comforting hymn because the wind must be blowing pretty damn hard before the shrouds begin to hum. It's a frightening sound. [Laughter] A touch of rum, I find, is another effective soporific. Instead of losing my tongue with rum, it puts me right to sleep and I wake up feeling wonderful. I can't see any bad effects from it.

ORSON: There are none once you get older. The doctors all say that except for me. I can't take it. I'm a little diabetic. I no longer drink or smoke.

ROGER: What do you mean you don't smoke? You never have a cigar out of your mouth.

ORSON: I haven't smoked a cigar for a year and a half.

ROGER: In front of a camera you still do, don't you? It's a prop?

ORSON: Yes. I use it as a prop, but I don't smoke it. Cigar smoking is really not a vice like cigarettes. It's a pleasure. Just one more pleasure you give up through the twilight years.

ROGER: Tell me about your current projects. Tell me something uplifting.

ORSON: Remember *The Cradle Will Rock* with Marc Blitzstein? We moved from the Maxine Elliott Theatre to the Venice Theatre on the opening night. We're moving ahead to make a movie about that night.

ROGER: Wonderful.

ORSON: I thought at first I couldn't do it. Then, I thought it would be all right if I came on as myself at the beginning and said, "There's a character in the story called Orson Welles and I don't know him at all. I only have some of his memories, but I really don't know what he was like. So I'm not taking any position in the matter." On that basis, I think I might get by with it. I don't play myself. A twenty-two-year-old actor plays Orson Welles. I was actually twenty-one when it started. The production began on my birthday. Everybody in that theatre was twenty years older than I.

ROGER: The story of staging *Cradle* has real possibilities.

ORSON: Houseman has taken over the entire production and pretended that he did it all, so this is a way to stop that. He produced something in New York last year called *Houseman/Welles Cradle Will Rock*. Pale, painful fare. Now he's going to be on Home Box Office giving a speech about how it happened, and I can shut him up with the movie.

ROGER: Good. But, of course, like all the projects you did together, he was by your side, there's no doubt about that.

Cover of Orson's screenplay, *The Cradle Will Rock*.

ORSON: Not in that production. No, Virginia was. She was at my side and he was biting his fingernails wondering whether we were doing the right thing. It's a good idea. At the same time, I don't dare screw up *Lear*. I'm trying to keep everybody happy. I hope I can live through it. It's a tremendous program of work, but it's better than lying around and wondering whether I have enough energy to get out of bed and direct, much less ride a crane. Actually, the need to ride a crane has been eliminated. You have a TV monitor and it shows every inch of your movie as it's being shot, where everybody is, the lights and everything.

ROGER: That was such a wonderful time in your life. I'm so glad that you're going to recreate it on film.

ORSON: I'm trying hard to pull it off. I have a very strong argument because I am quietly rewriting it to make it more amusing, and I have the infallible argument when I say, "That's what happened." But, of course, it isn't entirely what happened. I'm remembering it the way it ought to have been. [Laughter]

ROGER: That's very exciting.

ORSON: What I have decided to do is take the heavy left wing atmosphere out of it because that just loses the audience. We were set to open with a thirty-two-piece orchestra and a huge production when the government put padlocks on the theatre doors, and there was the audience, standing outside. I remember all that. We're going be faithful to what actually happened. Within hours of the lockout, we found another theatre, the Venice, and walked the whole audience twenty blocks to the new venue. We put an upright piano on the stage. The union wouldn't allow the actors on the stage that night. They were sitting in the audience, and when their cue came, they stood up and acted with a spotlight on them. I had this very elaborate production with every set on rollers. I told Marc he shouldn't do an opera for the ladies' garment workers and the communist union. Instead, he should do it for *Vanity Fair, Vogue,* and *Harpers* audiences, and it should have no atmosphere of being a little labor opera. It should be a big Broadway show. Then, we were locked out of the Federal Theatre, which led to the birth of the Mercury Theatre.

ROGER: Yes, Hopkins—

ORSON: Was very much in favor of what we did. Though many politicians denounced me for having done *Faustus*, written by that well-known communist Christopher Marlowe.

ROGER: [Laughing] I don't know how *Faustus* could make
              you sound leftist.

ORSON: The Federal Theatre Project came under attack, if
              you recall, from the Dies House Un-American
              Activities Committee and the Hearst papers, to
              name a few, claiming it was a communist conspiracy.
              The hammer fell in the form of considerable
              governmental budget cuts just as *Cradle* was to
              open, at the height of the CIO's efforts to organize
              steel. Another reason for closing us was that,
              unlike most WPA plays, we were going to be on
              Broadway, which opponents feared would attract
              considerable attention.

ROGER: How right they were, but I don't get the *Faustus*
              connection.

ORSON: Faust was running the day before we opened
              Cradle. It had run for five months and had been
              denounced in Congress by a number of anti-
              Roosevelt people as a communist play. Just as
              they violently attacked *Voodoo Macbeth*, they
              denounced *Cradle*. They succeeded in closing the
              play as a federal project. They legislated against the
              Federal Theatre and, in fact, the whole WPA project.

ROGER: There certainly was a lot of prejudice against the
              WPA. I remember Noble Hill once complaining
              that, "You never can get lost in Chicago because
              the moss grows on the north side of the WPA
              workers," which was so cruel because the WPA,
              the CCC boys, did a lot of good. Of course, there
              was probably a lot of loafing on the job.

ORSON: There was that. But, the other part of it was
              wonderful. For a couple of years, we had a national
              theatre.

ROGER: What did you receive as a salary?

ORSON: I never received a dollar. I'm the only person who ever put money into a government project illegally. [Laughter] I was the only celebrity in the WPA who would drive a Rolls or race down the Hudson River in a motorboat to rehearsals. Yes. I was The Wonder of the Western World at twenty-two [laughs], a legitimate star.

ROGER: Weren't you just? Horty and I saw you in *Cradle* a few weeks later. I never witnessed a more impassioned performance or audience.

ORSON: Yes, Marc, Will Geer, and so many in the cast were genuine zealots who inspired their fellow true believers to flood the theatre week after week.

ROGER: It was an electrifying evening of theatre, oh so long ago. You kid me about obsessing over being old. But wait until you approach ninety. My God, you're young compared to me.

ORSON: Nobody is young. We start dying when we're born. That's why I kid you about your ruminations on age. Just this afternoon, I was writing about this irony in my *Cradle* script. At the time I was directing *Cradle*, I became fascinated with cycles, and began believing in seven-year cycles. I suddenly realized that when you reach a certain age, you cease being interested in cycles because the only thing that's interesting about a cycle is the future. When you arrive at a point where a seven-year cycle going forward is likely to include agonizing pain, increased loneliness, all the other unpleasant surprises of old age, the whole business of seven-year cycles loses its grip [laughs].

ROGER: Yes, it's best to take one day at a time and pray that you will wake in the morning with most of your facilities in adequate repair. So, you're currently working on your script?

ORSON: Oh, yes, I'm writing it, and I have a deal for which I have absolute artistic control including the final cut.

ROGER: Wonderful.

ORSON: I've been researching that period of my life. It mystifies me. It's a very strange thing to write about yourself, to write a work of fiction about yourself, because you realize that there are many things you don't know. There's a letter from Marc Blitzstein to me that I had totally forgotten, in which he thanks me for something wonderful I had done for him, and how I had improved his script. He ends by saying, "We know who our enemies are, but we will triumph in the end." If the audience has the sensitivities of a Sherlock Holmes, they can go back over the movie and figure out what my troubles were, you know what I mean? [Laughter] But I never show Houseman doing anything. That must have been what Marc Blitzstein was talking about, "We know who our enemies are." That was a period when Virginia was most hot about Houseman. I remember it was a matinee in my dressing room when she said, "I've never said this to you, but you've got to understand how much this man hates you."

ROGER: Well, he was jealous as hell.

ORSON: He's spent forty years hating me. He's made a career of it, but she was so right. Oja says that I mustn't read his books because they would upset me. I just ask her what he says about this or that, so I don't say something that he can refute. But back to *Cradle*. I'm turning Virginia into the leading heroine of the world and I'm sure she'll be happy about it. I'm giving her big scenes. She's a leading lady. That'll be a surprise to folks who know her today, to see what her life was like in the late '30s. She's the greatest girl in New York. It's the way to make me look bad, to portray Virginia as the virtuous wife, so she's the Virgin Mary. [Laughter]

ROGER: That's quite a bit of fiction, too. She was quite a gal, but she wasn't the Virgin Mary.

ORSON: [Laughing] Oh, no, that's right, but she was a virgin when I met her at Todd, one of the only ones I can remember. Virgins have that sort of look about them, and, before long, that look vanishes and so do the virgins.

ROGER: That reminds me about our summer theatre festival in Woodstock, when the mothers of the nubile aspiring school-age actresses said to Horty, "We wouldn't leave our daughters if it weren't for you."

ORSON: [Uproarious laughter]

ROGER: Horty had to spend all her nights trying to keep them virgins.

ORSON: [Still laughing] Pretty hard to do during the hot months. [More laughter] There are some very surprising people I've known who have told me that they were twenty-two or something when they married and both of them were virgins. It's astonishing.

Orson, Louise Prussing, Hilton Edwards, Constance Heron, and Micheál mac Liammóir relaxing at the Todd pool during the Todd Theatre Festival.

Micheál mac Liammóir, Louise Prussing, and nineteen-year-old Orson as Claudius, King of Denmark in Act V of the Todd Theatre Festival production of *Hamlet*.

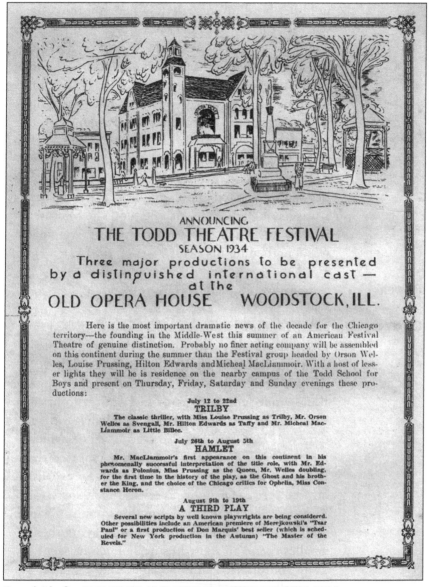

Broadside for THE TODD THEATRE FESTIVAL SEASON 1934

ROGER: Well, there used to be a premium placed on virginity.

ORSON: Losing it, losing the maidenhead, seems to be the first task of a young woman today. She can then hold her head up in society. When you think of what that used to mean. My God, at Todd, I had a couple of very hot love affairs with several young ladies in Woodstock at off-campus trysting spots, with barking and yelling and all that. [Laughing] Meaningful. It included everything but penetration. The maiden fair had to remain a maiden until the wedding day. Virgins, where are they now? They're an endangered species. I had a girlfriend years ago, she's still around, beautiful still, and she was being bedded by a noted choreographer at the same time I was having an affair with her and she told me that he was going to a doctor on Fifth Avenue who was lengthening his penis.

ROGER: Surgically?

ORSON: No, by pulling it somehow. That diminished my fortitude because I thought, if this guy has the moxie to have his prick enlarged, I really don't deserve her, he does and he married her. [Laughter] I know one fellow, an actor in Spain, who has a real problem because it's too big. He has difficulty entering. He's very Spanish, very macho. [Much laughter] It was a real problem. He reported that he was too big to perform and that all his exhaustive efforts were for naught. Everybody felt sorry for him. I've always admired one thing about Chaplin, who was famous in Hollywood for having the smallest penis in show business. Then he went away and married and had eight children after he was well into middle age, which must have silenced a lot of scurrilous laughter in the locker room.

ROGER: Who was the young woman he married?

ORSON: The daughter of Eugene O'Neill. A very nice girl.

ROGER: Oona.

ORSON: Yes. When she came to Hollywood, she was my girlfriend for a time. I used to tell fake fortunes as a way of ingratiating myself, and I told her that she would meet and marry Charles Chaplin.

ROGER: No kidding?

ORSON: Yes. I did it logically. It wasn't a stroke of clairvoyance. She so obviously needed a father, and had been talking about being infatuated with Leopold Stokowski. The more time we spent together, I could see she was going for me, and I was aware that it was just a case of a girl hunting in Hollywood for an intellectual, a substitute for her father who had totally neglected her, and who was sort of a genius. And I thought, well, who's a genius in Hollywood, who's at liberty. I mentioned Chaplin to her, and, by God, she met and married him.

ROGER: That's fascinating.

ORSON: She had a pretty rough time with him, I think. During their last years in Switzerland, he became irrational. He used to lock her up when he would go out of the house to keep the fellows away from her.

ROGER: I've forgotten the details of your run-in with him over the film, *Monsieur Verdoux*.

ORSON: That was on the credits. I came up with the idea of the film, based on the notorious Henri Landru, known in France as "Bluebeard." He was considered a "family man," when, in fact, he was a philanderer and murderer of ten women. Between 1915 and

1919, Landru placed advertisements in newspapers enticing widows with the prospect of marriage. After winning them over, he'd rob, kill, and incinerate them. He knew no shame. Throughout the month-long trial, Landru was supercilious and unrepentant. It took only a couple of hours for the jury to pronounce him guilty on all counts, and he was sentenced to death. Two months later, the sentence was carried out. Just before his execution, he rejected the traditional last Mass and the time-honored final glass of brandy, and knelt before the guillotine without ever a word of apology or regret. I wanted to make a film with Charlie as the killer. He bought the idea of the film, but he wanted to star and direct it himself. He based his film on my screenplay outline. It wasn't really a run-in, he just behaved strangely. I never had an argument with him about it, never a bad word. I just was badly treated by him, that's all.

ROGER: You didn't have a lawsuit?

ORSON: No, I wouldn't do that. Hang on. I'm signing checks hoping that they won't bounce. I've never done less business as a commercial speaker. It's been a very bad year.

ROGER: Your new project ought to liven things up.

ORSON: I have to turn down another job, which would have given me a million bucks. That always happens.

ROGER: I don't know why you have to turn it down, but I'll take your word for it.

ORSON: It was an acting job that would have taken me away from my pending projects. Did I tell you that I can barely sign my name anymore since being plagued by nerve damage in my right hand?

ROGER: How about the typewriter?

ORSON: I can still do it with the one finger. I can write
Orson without much of a problem, but writing
Welles turns out very strange. [Offstage to Freddie]
Freddie, go to lunch, will you? [Continues speaking
to Roger] The only slight consolation is that I have
a great excuse for my diminished sleight-of-hand
abilities. I don't know whether I will draw again.
The forced march of time ushers in increasing
ailments and the prospect of creeping senility.
There's nothing to recommend growing old,
gracefully or otherwise. The script is a little more
than half done. I'll send you what I have when
I've completed a bit more.

ROGER: Great.

ORSON: [Offstage to an assistant.] I'll see you before you
go. [Resumes conversation with Roger] I was talking
to my lady and she's just left. Now we're alone. She
presented me with all these checks because she's
going away on holiday.

ROGER: I don't know whether you'd want to do it, but it's
possible to give somebody—

ORSON: Power of Attorney?

ROGER: Yes.

ORSON: I've been burned too many times. No matter how
honest they are or how limited the Power of Attorney,
it just scares me. I've lost such fortunes of money
from folks who were allegedly representing my best
interests.

ROGER: That's right. You're in a different position than I was, a poor schoolman always wondering whether there was much in the bank and no secretary was tempted to dip into something sweet.

ORSON: I didn't get little secretaries. They were always the big brainy fellows who were going to set me up. Get my affairs in order. [Laughing] The only mistake I made in my youth is the mistake every actor, director, and writer made in those years. I sold my work outright and didn't keep a piece of it. You know what I could have made on *Kane*? It's just unthinkable. *Touch of Evil* reopened in Paris last week in five theatres. People are standing in line for blocks to get in.

ROGER: You don't get a dime?

ORSON: No, I don't get a dime, but it's nice that it's being seen.

ROGER: Yes, of course it is.

ORSON: I've never received a dime from royalties. I've spent my own money all my life to be a director.

ROGER: Well I know.

ORSON: But, I'll get paid a percentage with *Lear*, if they manage to get all the money. I'm meeting them in about three weeks in France. The fellow who will finance *Cradle* came to see me, and he phones every couple of days. He's after me to send my script to Lardner, who wrote the original script.

ROGER: This is the young Ring Lardner?

ORSON: Yes, he's the son of Ring Lardner, one of the
screenwriters who went to jail during the U.S.
Congress witch-hunt for subversives. He was
one of the "Hollywood Ten." He's just the wrong
man for this script because his draft is full of the
intensity of the true believers still passionate in
the thrall of Communism. It's just the wrong note
to strike because the point of the story is really
not the threat of Communism in New York City.
[Laughing]. While doing some research, I discovered that there was a meeting in New York City,
headed by Harry Hopkins at the Hopkins Hotel, a
year before they closed down our theatre, in which
they decided on the date to close the WPA. Now,
that's just incredible. Another thing I discovered is
what turned Marc Blitzstein to Communism. He
had been married and his wife, Eva, had just died
before we met. She had a Communist mission. His
vision of Communism was a consequence of his
wife's political passion and it had to do with having
lost his love, you see? His wife, a Communist,
was the missionary who converted him. Therefore,
Marc's extraordinary devotion to a pure form of
Communism was really an aspect of his mourning
for his wife. He seemed completely non-sexual at
the time. Marc existed in and was defined by his
work. It wasn't until later that it occurred to
Virginia and me that he might be homosexual
because he was deeply in love with his wife.
I'm going to put that revelation in the script this
afternoon. The depositions that were taken at the
end of the WPA included everybody that was
connected with the Federal Theatre. They have
nothing to say that isn't interesting to me. There
is an actor I know who doesn't think much of
me, who goes on for three pages saying, "I've
never heard Orson Welles raise his voice or say
any unkind thing to an actor in my life."

In May, 1933, after returning from his success in Ireland, while collaborating with Skipper on *Everybody's Shakespeare*, my grandfather, who was directing a Todd production of the Bard's *Twelfth Night* to be performed for the Chicago Drama League, invited Orson to provide assistance that included painting the "picture book" sets, and proffering acting advice to the cast. My fifteen-year-old father was cast as Sir Andrew Aguecheek, and my fifteen-year-old mother as Viola (Cesairo). In Act III: Scene 4, Sir Andrew is provoked into dueling with Viola, disguised as Cesario. On being directed by Welles, which he was frequently, my father reflected forty years later, "At Todd, Orson had an aura about him that few questioned. It took a very firm, experienced adult to not be overwhelmed by Welles. We students were in his theatre and we did what he wanted. We did it quite well as a matter of fact, because he left absolutely no latitude, no tolerance for self-expression. In every scene, he told you where to stand, where to move, and how to deliver your lines with specific intonations. He choreographed all his plays tightly, and the results were amazing, absolutely amazing."

ROGER: Well, that's a little overdoing it.

ORSON: No, it's true.

Heartbreak House **opened at the Mercury Theatre, April 29, 1938.**

ROGER: Really?

ORSON: Yes, you're thinking of my directing the Todd boys. I do all my mean talk to the people behind the camera. Anybody who has to perform in front of the public is treated with great deference. I take it out on poor assistant directors, and usually for the benefit of the actors, to show them what they could be getting.

ROGER: It's a defensive position.

ORSON: [Laughing] Yes. But, you can't play around with delicate instruments that have the real stuff for a stage play or a movie.

ROGER: Is he among the quick?

ORSON: Yes, very much so, and a successful actor.

ROGER: That isn't your old friend who's on TV that I used to think was quite a guy.

ORSON: Vincent Price?

ROGER: Vincent Price.

ORSON: No, it wasn't Vincent.

ROGER: He was in *Heartbreak House*, wasn't he?

ORSON: Yes, and not very happy in the role. He was particularly vexed that he was required to stand still and listen to other actors talking at great length, as actors do in Shaw. He said, "Orson, I have to have something to do." I responded, "Well, Vincent, the rest of us are standing still and listening to this speech and we're not unhappy about it. Suppose we were all doing something, it would sound and look like the monkey house." And he said, "Well, I have to have something to do." So, thinking to shame him, on the opening night I said, "Vincent, eat an apple." And on opening night I heard, "crunch, crunch." He was eating an apple. [Laughter] He's very bitter against me I hear because he believed that he should have played great leading roles like Hamlet, and in the Mercury, he didn't get those roles. He thinks I destroyed his entire career. [Laughter] I don't think he felt this way until later in his life when he had to find a reason why he was still making terrible horror movies at the age of sixty. I was on a talk show with him two or three years ago, and he said to me, during the commercial break, "Isn't it wonderful, here we are together, the two most wonderful voices in the American Theatre." [Uproarious laughter] I'll talk to you soon.

ROGER: Bye.

[Lights dim.]

ACT TWO
SCENE TWO
OCTOBER 4, 1984
BORING YOU NEVER WILL BE

Interior of Orson and Roger's libraries. Roger's telephone rings and he picks up the receiver.

ORSON: Roger, how are you?

ROGER: What's new in your world?

ORSON: I did a pilot for a TV show the other day, which I hope sells because it's an easy job and it's quite a lot of money. They're calling it *Scene of the Crime*. It's not very elevating, but we'll see.

ROGER: When will it air?

ORSON: In a couple of weeks, I guess. This is a half-hour mystery program, something like Hitchcock, except the audience is supposed to determine who did it. As the host, I provide the audience clues and a touch of levity. If the audience is clever, they should be able to figure out "who-done-it." I hope it's picked up because it's not the kind of TV job that would tie me up for all of the year. I can do five shows in one day. I'm only on for a page-and-a-half. The rest is all off-screen. It's an ideal grocery-paying show.

ROGER: We'll hope.

ORSON: I have to hope. I've never had any luck with TV, so I'm pessimistic. I used to think I was made for the medium, but the medium consists of such total junk.

ROGER: [Laughing] Well, I remember years ago you remarked that there just wasn't enough material available to have consistently good programming.

ORSON: It isn't because they run out of good stuff. No, the networks don't try to provide quality programming. [Laughter] They're interested in young viewers who have the money. I don't know why young people seem to like me, and crowd in whenever I speak, because I never thought I would appeal to them. I've always worked with an audience, which I conceived as being mature—a lot of dead heads from the point of view of the young. [Laughter]

ROGER: This prompts me to again plead for you to tape your Shakespearian lectures for young and old audiences. I still hope that we can get our Shakespearian stuff on cassettes with your discussing each of the plays.

ORSON: A very well-known Shakespearian scholar in England has translated Shakespeare. He's run right through most of the best-known plays. Wherever a modern audience does not know a word, he has supplied another one that they will know. It's just like the recent recasting of the *Bible.* You hear it and it sounds awful. So, one doesn't know what gallimaufry means. One can always open a dictionary. The distinguished Cambridge don is ruining the meter.

ROGER: If the meter's gone, then what's left?

ORSON: What's left? I saw the don not long ago on public television. The program, like so much of public television, featured talking heads struggling tediously to remain perpetually "balanced" and, as a result, it comes out like skim milk. [Laughter] That's the smart thing about English television. It's openly partisan. They let people go on and on. And they don't bother trying to make it balanced. Whoever is on represents his point of view and away he goes and it's so much more stimulating, even if you don't agree with a word anybody's saying. We not only have to have a happy ending to every story, but every startling statement must be sweetened at the end. If you say that three-fourths of the people in the world are hungry, you then have to say that a commission has been formed to end hunger. [Laughter] By the way, whatever happened to the piece you wanted me to help place in *Newsweek*?

ROGER: I couldn't get it boiled down to the proper length. My argument, if you remember, is that there are a lot of folks like me who are over sixty-five, have ample money, and shouldn't be taking Social Security because other folks, in true economic want, need it a lot more, and the government should cut off payments to people who exceed a certain income level.

ORSON: That's a compelling argument.

ROGER: A number of people I've shown it to scream that no one will agree with me. Social Security has become an engrained entitlement. If anyone even whispers, "Let's reconsider eligibility requirement," people scream foul. Nobody, it appears, wants to give it up.

ORSON: Except you and me.

ROGER: Another essay I want to write deals with the difficulties Latinos are experiencing in contemporary America.

ORSON: That's another timely topic. Somebody said to me the other day that because of the Latino population increase out here, he was worried about California becoming Quebec and wanting independence. I said, "Well then, they'd only be asking for what we stole from them."[Laughter]

ROGER: That's right.

ORSON: But they're a funny bunch those Latinos, because they insist on teaching school partly in Spanish. I can't agree with that. It's paralyzing the kids. It's not holding their culture together. The Hispanics around the country don't seem to want to speak English. That's where they differ from the Chinese, the Japanese, the Irish, the Germans, the Czechs, and the Poles. All these people, who came in various waves of migration, wanted to be part of America. The trouble with our neighbors to the south is they want to go on being what they were, which is bound to make it harder for them. Compensatory educational programs and lowering university entrance requirements for minorities hurts, rather than helps, in the final analysis. I know a young fellow who got the highest marks in his class at his university. He was up for a scholarship and it was given instead to a black who received poorer marks. I think that was wrong, don't you?

ROGER: I'm afraid it is.

ORSON: If a black wants to have dignity, he shouldn't be accepting that kind of a handout. Phones are ringing. Thank you for calling.

ROGER: Thank you for being. We'll talk soon. Bye.

ORSON: Bye.

[Lights dim.]

Interiors of Roger and Orson's libraries, October 5, 1984. Orson picks up telephone receiver and dials Roger. The telephone rings three times in Roger's dark library with no response, which activates his answering system.

ORSON: Roger, when I spoke with you yesterday, I would have liked the conversation to have been longer, but you seemed restless. Was I boring? Most people on the telephone bore me.

I tried to tell you how much I have enjoyed reading your new chapters of *Time and Chance* and, like its predecessor, how well written it is. Do you realize that this is true? Your prose has always reflected so much of your own personality, which is a real accomplishment. Few professional writers manage a truly individual voice. It isn't enough to say you have lost none of your cunning. The truth is you have improved. You quote someone's criticism of your youthful work to the effect that it was somewhat "belabored."

My recollection of what might be called your Middle Period is of a certain tendency to the ornate. In my own youth, of course, my every expression was in some way an imitation of you, and I still recognize a lamentable bias in the direction of the be-spangled and overly acrobatic for which I am happy to accord you the fullest blame. I have not improved in this (or much else) worth mentioning. You, on the other hand, have truly found a voice, so that your paragraphs seem to reach the ear even as they meet the eye.

One can only criticize the length. That is to say, the lack of it. I do truly believe that a full-scale version of the same thing would be a real publishing success. There would be generous quotations from those ancestral journals. Come to think of it, a well-edited collection of just those documents, the ones you speak of, but don't show, would be well worth serious printing. Please realize what a treasure you have produced. If we are to have it only in nugget form, we are still much in your debt.

Your ever-worshipful Orson.

[Lights dim.]

Interiors of Roger and Orson's libraries, October 6, 1984. Roger picks up telephone receiver and dials Orson. The telephone rings three times in Orson's dark library with no response, which activates his answering system.

ROGER: Orson, sorry I missed your call yesterday. Boring you never will be. Exasperating, you can be on occasion. For instance, in today's mail, I received an envelope from you with, of all things, a check! Frantic search for a message. Nothing! As for your damn money, in frustration, I tore up the check and threw it in a wastebasket. Good God, Orson, the one thing you don't owe me, and never will owe me, is money. It was a very long time ago when we last spent a dime on you. Dim memory recalls maybe a fifty-dollar jalopy to start you and

Virginia on your way to New York. Hortense may have, in filial fondness, even financed a wedding ring then. I've forgotten details. What I'll never forget is that, even back then, we were deep in your debt for your being you and being part of our family and, since that time, we've taken, and taken, and taken financial help from you. Must I make a list? If you've forgotten, we never will. First there was ten grand toward Todd's scholarship fund plus an equal amount through your influence from Charlie Lederer. Then royalties on our Shakespeare books which you refused. On that venture, I had merely the idea plus authorship of the introductory material. You did the rest.

[Lights dim.]

Shortly after Orson's *War of the Worlds* broadcast, he met a group of Todd boys in New York City and drove with them on Todd's "school on wheels," Big Bertha, to Washington, D.C., providing an informal seminar on the theatre and broadcasting.

ACT I

Scene VI

A Street

The original description of this scene is "The sea-coast," as which, occasionally, it is still presented. But as the succeeding short scene, for obvious reasons, is run right into this without drawing a curtain, perhaps the best description is "A street in the suburbs—on the road to the Duke's palace." It can be a painted drop, plain curtains, or as elaborate as the facilities of your stage will permit.

Sebastian enters, closely followed by Antonio.

Sebastian is Viola's twin brother whom she imagines to be drowned. He resembles her very closely and is dressed in an identical costume to the one which she is wearing in her disguise as page-boy to Orsino; usually the national dress of Greece. Although scholars have attempted to identify the mythical Illyria with what is now Dalmatia, play-producers, and perhaps very correctly, have persisted in costuming all the Illyrians in the English clothing of Shakespeare's period. But the twins, besides looking alike, should look like foreigners.

Antonio is a Sea-Captain who has picked up Sebastian after the wreck. He is a big, strong-looking man, warm-hearted and impulsive.

Antonio. Will you not that I go with you?

Sebastian. (*Stopping Center and turning to face him*) By your patience, no.

Antonio. Let me yet know of you whither you are bound.

Sebastian. No, sooth, sir: my determinate voyage is mere extravagancy. But I perceive in you so excellent a touch of modesty, that you will not extort from me what I am willing to keep in; therefore it charges me in manners the rather to express myself. You must know of me then, Antonio, my name is Sebastian. My father was that Sebastian of Messaline, whom I know you have heard of. He left behind him myself and a sister, both born in an hour: If the heavens had been pleased, would we had so ended! but you, sir, altered that; (*Brokenly*) for some hour before you took me from the breach of the sea was my sister drowned.

Antonio. Alas the day!

"Will you not that I go with you."

From *Everybody's Shakespeare*, *Twelfth Night*, Act I, Scene VI

ACT TWO
SCENE THREE
OCTOBER 29, 1984
I REMEMBER BITS AND PIECES OF
EVERYTHING YOU DO

Roger in his library, Orson reading a manuscript while sitting on the toilet in his home in Los Angeles. He puts the manuscript down on the sink to his left, picks up a telephone on the wall above the sink and dials. Roger's telephone rings and he picks it up.

ROGER: Hello.

ORSON: So, how are you?

ROGER: I'm doing very well [pause] for an old guy. [Laughs] Did you get the book I sent you?

ORSON: That's why I'm calling, to thank you. It's just wonderful. It's very entertaining. I keep reading things I know, which makes me feel smart, and then finding things I never knew. [Addresses Freddie offstage] Go ahead, Freddie. Ah, I was shouting at Freddie. I'm sitting on the toilet. I've got extensions everywhere, and, unfortunately, right in the bathroom because inevitably, when I'm in the shower I receive all the important calls. People pleading, "We'd like you to come to 'The Friends of Ronnie Dinner' tomorrow night." [Laughter] Reagan's weaker than he's ever been. We must hope that he doesn't start a little war somewhere because you always vote for the guy who's winning the war.

ROGER: Yes, for after all, who won Grenada? [Laughs]

ORSON: All he needs is one little war.

ROGER: It was a noble victory.

ORSON: Yes, a famous victory. I'm not very interested in the Caribbean anymore because it's become a land of high-rises like the rest of the world, but when I was a kid it struck me as one of the most romantic places in the world. Not as romantic as the Dalmatian coast, which you may have forgotten, but you used to talk about.

ROGER: I was so anxious to sail those waters, but never did.

ORSON: Your enthusiasm stuck with me. I didn't know what the Dalmatian coast was. [Laughs] It sounded so wonderful when you talked about it. Absolutely magical.

ROGER: Speaking of the Caribbean reminds me of a wonderful Wendell Phillips oration that all of us had to learn in my youth, *Toussaint L'Ouverture*.

ORSON: Toussaint L'Ouverture, the black Napoleon, yes.

ROGER: It was a great oration that Noble Hill insisted all Todd students master—"*You think me a fanatic tonight, for you read history not with your eyes but your prejudices. But fifty years hence when Truth gets a hearing, the Muse of History will put Phocion for the Greek, and Brutus for the Roman, Hampden for England, Fayette for France, choose Washington as the bright, consummate flower of our earlier civilization, and John Brown, the ripe flower of our noon-day, then dipping her pen in the sunlight, will write in the clear blue above them all, the name of the soldier, the statesman, the martyr, Toussaint L'Ouverture."*

ORSON: Yes, I remember you doing it for me once. I also remember your reciting a large portion of Ingersoll's Nomination of James Blaine, and returning to my room, memorizing it that evening, and declaiming to you and Horty the next day.

ROGER: I remember, *"James G. Blaine marched down the halls of the American Congress..."*

ORSON: Yes, *"Like an armed warrior, like a plumed knight, James G. Blaine marched down the halls of the American Congress and threw his shining lance full and fair against the brazen foreheads of the defamers of his country and the malingers of his honor. For the Republican party, to desert this gallant leader now, is as though an army should desert their general upon the field of battle."*

ROGER: Perfect. How do you remember such things? [Both laugh]

ORSON: *"Gentlemen of the convention, in the name of the great Republic, the only republic that ever existed upon this earth; in the name of all her defenders and of all her supporters; in the name of all her soldiers living; in the name of all her soldiers dead upon the field of battle, and in the name of those who perished in the skeleton clutch of famine at Andersonville and Libby, whose sufferings he so vividly remembers, Illinois, Illinois nominates for the next President of this country that prince of parliamentarians, that leader of leaders, James G. Blaine."*

ROGER: Amazing. How do you recall with perfect clarity this antique oration?

ORSON: Because I heard you doing it, and I remember bits and pieces of everything you do. Now, what I'm calling you for while on the toilet is to ask what psalm or proverb contains "Though I speak with the tongues of men and of angels, and have not love, I am become as sounding brass, or a tinkling cymbal."

ROGER: That's Corinthians 13, I believe.

ORSON: "When I was a child, I spake as a child, I understood as a child, I thought as a child: but when I became a man, I put away childish things."

ROGER: "For now we see through a glass, darkly; but then face to face: now I know in part; but then shall I know even as also I am known. And now abideth faith, hope, charity, these three; but the greatest of these is charity." Yes, the First Epistle of Paul the Apostle to the Corinthians.

ORSON: Once again you come to my instant aid. I've got a Gideon *Bible* I stole from a hotel somewhere. I don't know what sin that is. I've used this well-thumbed *Bible* to read passages on TV and at people's dinners.

ROGER: I'm sure you have.

ORSON: I've spread the word.

ROGER: You have spread the word and done a great job of it, [Laughing] and you could make a fortune very simply, in a day or two, by giving some readings from the *Bible*, mainly about Paul. Everybody is crazy about the *Bible* and the man who founded the Christian religion.

ORSON: Producing such recordings can be done quite cheaply and sold on local television stations. These stations go into business with you. They provide free commercials for your product if you give them a piece of the action. Therefore, you don't need much capital investment. People send in their money and receive their purchase plus a bonus. It never works unless you give them something free besides the featured item. I received all that information from the expert, you, the old advertising man. In other words, if I'm old Uncle Bill, the cowboy singer, and I'm advertising my long-playing record, I'll send you my long-playing record, plus you will receive a multi-colored necklace or a baby doll signed by Uncle Bill. Without these incentives, the product won't move, and you have to emphasize that it's "Just for this one time only."

ROGER: That's right. "For a limited time."

ORSON: It's the oldest advertising gimmick in the world. Did you work in your callow youth for Sears or Montgomery Ward?

ROGER: Monkey Wards.

ORSON: They were more honest.

ROGER: We looked down on Sears. Monkey Wards was the originator of the mail order universe.

ORSON: Oh, they were?

ROGER: Yes. Sears was just an upstart.

ORSON: Sears and Montgomery Ward cleaned up their act, but much of the early advertising was based on sex.

Women in their underwear were such a revelation to the boys on the farm.

ROGER: There was a definite touch of the salacious in their approach. The thinking was, if you're going to sell a corset, you've got to show a bit of what's under it. You remember the tale of my talented and drunken cousin, Jack Rogers?

ORSON: The free-spirited writer?

ROGER: Yes. Anecdotes of Jack were endless. There was praise for him and the phantom lady he created, Elizabeth Harlan Young.

ORSON: I forget the details.

ROGER: The 1912 Montgomery Ward catalogue promoted in screaming, all cap headlines, ELIZABETH HARLAN YOUNG IS HERE TO HELP YOU. Jack was the voice of this imaginary character that proffered advice to the fairer sex throughout the country. The conceit worked financial wonders for a year. Then all hell began to break loose. Farm ladies began descending on the corporate office in Chicago by the hundreds and then thousands seeking Elizabeth's sexual counsel rather than wardrobe wisdom. The mail to "Elizabeth" was so voluminous it required a sizeable staff of scribes to respond. One classic line that comes to mind is something like, "Only we women can know the seductive delight to be found in a silky kimono after a bath." [Laughter]

ORSON: Little wonder the ladies felt they could confide to such a kindred spirit.

ROGER: After a year, the company decided it best to bid

adieu to Elizabeth. The 1913 catalogue announced to their faithful customers, "We're sorry; Elizabeth Harlan Young has left the business."

ORSON: Roger, reluctantly, I must put an end to our call. I have to go to an important dinner, which has to do with money.

ROGER: Good luck and goodbye.

ORSON: Bye.

[Lights dim.]

The Magnificent Ambersons

"The people who controlled RKO destroyed the last reel and a half. The gaggle of Hollywood press predicted that Kane would flop and after Ambersons, I'd be tossed out of town."

The Magnificent Ambersons

"What's so remarkable about the original script you sent me years ago is that, in 1942, it lyrically prophesied so accurately and affectingly a future America beset by a number of the environmental problems that we struggle with today."

ACT TWO
SCENE FOUR
NOVEMBER 3, 1984
STANDING UP IN A HAMMOCK

Interior of Orson and Roger's libraries. Orson's telephone rings and he answers it.

ROGER: Orson?

ORSON: Hello, Roger? Did you get the first draft of the script?

ROGER: No.

ORSON: I'll send you another. How are you?

ROGER: I'm grand, and I'm excited that you're going ahead so fast on *Cradle*. The schedule you're setting for yourself is dizzying, but you always do things the hard way.

ORSON: You know what the hard way of making love is, don't you?

ROGER: [Laughing] No, I don't.

ORSON: Standing up in a hammock. [Laughter] Good title for my book, I thought.

ROGER: Exactly, a wonderful description of your life.

ORSON: Isn't it! [More laughter]

ROGER: The ABC morning show interviewed the actress who is going to play Virginia. Who is she?

ORSON: Her name is Amy Irving, and she's quite a star now. She's been in two or three pictures in which she starred. She's well known to all the younger moviegoers, those under sixty. I'd never heard of her until I saw a film she made recently. Strangely enough, her uncle, Richard Irving, directed the last three *Scene of the Crime* episodes I did. He's a very nice man, which is hard to find among the hacks that work on these TV shows.

ROGER: Well, that's good because sometimes you fight with directors.

ORSON: No, I don't fight with directors, just producers. The director has to do something, the producer doesn't do anything. They're difficult to work with because they have no function. They have to create one for themselves. It usually ends up as mischief making. It's a very important job with no function. [Laughter]

ROGER: Nice job if you can get it, it appears.

ORSON: Producers have a three-hour lunch, maybe drop by the set for a second after lunch. That's their working day. And, they always have to get themselves "involved" with creative input. They always say that movies are a collective art form, but they aren't. It's a dictatorship whenever a movie is good. If it isn't a dictatorship, then the movie looks like every other movie. Somebody's signature has to be on it.

ROGER: That's certainly true with your work.

ORSON: The producers have to shut up. As I've mentioned, I have what's called the "final cut" in the *Cradle* contract. It's most important to me that the version that I cut is the one that goes out. I didn't have it for *Touch of Evil*, I didn't have—

ROGER: Nor for *Ambersons* that they bastardized.

ORSON: Not bastardized. The people who controlled RKO destroyed the last reel and a half. The gaggle of Hollywood press predicted that *Kane* would flop and after *Ambersons*, I'd be tossed out of town. I wasn't tossed, but I certainly wasn't embraced. It was almost four years before I was offered another director's job.

ROGER: *Ambersons* was just too dark and troubling for a public that wanted to be entertained and not enlightened.

ORSON: Yes, many in the preview audience at the Balboa Theatre, in Pasadena, were bothered for want of an effervescent, upbeat narrative.

ROGER: What's so remarkable about the original script you sent me years ago is that in 1942 it lyrically prophesied so accurately and affectingly a future America beset by a number of the environmental problems that we struggle with today. There are a couple of lines that have stuck because they are so timeless. As we see passengers on a streetcar, you comment, "The faster we're carried, the less time we have—"

ORSON: "To spare."

ROGER: Yes. And another when Eugene comments that automobiles "with all their speed forward may be a step backward in civilization."

ORSON: It's true. Man rarely takes the time to look back
           and appreciate his recent, much less ancient, past,
           which has helped define who we are. I don't know
           whether it'll be interesting because television rarely
           is; they cut you off so short. But I'm doing a live
           show tonight on Orwell's *1984*, and must leave
           shortly for the studio.

ROGER: Now that 1984 has arrived, in some ways, the
           world is even worse than he predicted.

ORSON: I think he was dead wrong.

ROGER: Tell me.

ORSON: Orwell was a fanatically dedicated independent
           socialist, and anti-Communist.

ROGER: Yes.

ORSON: Big Brother is really Stalin. You cannot read the
           book without seeing this. It's really an anti-Stalin
           book. That's my view. I think that where we have
           gone wrong is more perfectly expressed in Huxley's
           Brave New World about self-indulgence.

ROGER: That's right.

ORSON: Self-indulgence better defines our consumer
           society's collapse than Orwell's vision, which is a
           better description of life in the frozen depths of
           Russia than it is here. Orwell also leaves out the
           tremendous problem, the obvious one of enormous
           concern, which is the unthinkable pile of nuclear
           armaments.

ROGER: You don't think there's any chance for change in
          the USSR? We spent two weeks in Russia a decade
          ago and didn't sense there was much of an overt
          cry for change politically in Moscow. But, when
          we traveled along the Volga, we heard a good deal
          of *sotto voce* grumbling. It seemed to me that
          there's a good chance that they will overthrow
          that dictatorship one day.

ORSON: I don't know. I'm not too sanguine that in the
          short-term they can. Only the Ukrainians, along
          with an incredibly brave handful of intellectuals,
          stood up against the machine. You take them away
          and the only real dissidents are the Lithuanians,
          the Estonians, the Ukrainians, and all the people
          who don't think they're Russian. It's not hatred of
          the system because the people have never known
          anything else. It's the hatred of being under the
          heel of Moscow instead of Odessa. I fell into the
          great vat as a young man after the war believing
          that the world was going to become smaller and
          we were going to have one world. The truth is
          the world today is fragmented, much more than it
          was when I was a child at Todd. Then, there was
          one Spain and now there is Catalonia, the Basque,
          and Galicia, and they are three absolutely separate
          countries and they'll never be wed. There's the
          Irish question that will never be solved. There are
          the Serbs and the Croats who will never lie down
          together.

ROGER: We certainly live in fractious times. Before I forget,
          is this program live tonight and when does it air?

ORSON: It's at 7:30 my time, which means it's something
          like 10:30 your time. There are three of us talking.
          Irving Howe and the other is the bullfrog with the
          pipe, James Schlesinger, who was head of the CIA

for a while in the early '70s. I'm going to challenge him because I don't see how anybody could possibly have been the head of the CIA and have a non-prejudiced opinion about democracy. The tragic excuse for the secret apparatus is that it is needed to protect democracy. They are sustaining consumerist capitalism without any reference to democracy. It goes without saying that if you have a secret apparatus you are operating in direct opposition to everything that we understand about an open society.

ROGER: I look forward to your appearance on the tube.

ORSON: Television has a certain value because it is a kind of window on the world.

ROGER: I'm so glad you called. Thank God, you're still the most interesting guy in the world. So, if you let me know what you're doing—

ORSON: What I'm doing is sitting talking with my dearest and oldest friend.

ROGER: As am I.

ORSON: As always, it's a joy hearing your voice.

ROGER: Bye.

[Lights dim.]

ACT TWO
SCENE FIVE

NOVEMBER 8, 1984
MOST OLD PEOPLE ARE SUSTAINED
NOT BY LOVE, BUT BY A SENSE OF POWER

Interior of Orson and Roger's libraries. Orson's telephone rings.

ORSON: Hello.

ROGER: Well, tell me what happened to the *1984* television show. It didn't come on the night you indicated.

ORSON: It aired, but I was wrong about the night. It came on late Sunday night and early Monday morning. One of us was in Washington, another was in New York, and I was in Hollywood. We weren't much good, I think, because we all agreed with each other. We were terribly nice to each other, except before we went on air. I made a not terribly complimentary comment about Orwell. I really meant it to be a reference to his book, *1984*, and not about Orwell himself, and there was the great growling voice of Schlesinger disagreeing with me heartily.

Did I tell you that I'll be doing a reading with the symphony orchestra in Vienna? I can't afford not to go. I can't record it here; I have to perform before an audience in Vienna. Years ago, I offered to do a reading on a recording for Lenny Bernstein and the Philharmonic. He was indignant that I wouldn't come to New York. I did another reading with Yehudi Menuhin where I didn't have the orchestra and he was perfectly happy to lay it in. There's no reason why a recording can't be laid in. In fact, they use so many tracks today and can control it better if you're not there. But, conductors like to conduct. They like to point at the actor telling him when to speak and all that. That's the greatest source of personal power open to the human ego.

ROGER: Of course it is. You started playing with that egomania as a child director.

ORSON: Sure. But, whatever egomania may have infected my youthful directing pales by comparison to conductors. And, conductors never die, because when you go to work in the morning, there are 120 men doing everything you say. Such power is absolutely intoxicating. Very few old people get that amount of obedience. It's the only way to go. They never give up. Many thrive well into their 90s, and they depart the scene at that venerable age only if they are run over by a streetcar. My theory is that most old people are sustained not by love, because they don't get it, but by a sense of power. That's why they become despots in the old fashioned family of the old fashioned firm. The symphonic conductor has all those things going for him besides being applauded. Imagine. I only know one young conductor that I've worked with who hasn't made it into old age. He's a very talented and delightful one, an Italian, who has epilepsy, so he can only record. He can't perform before an audience. It's a terrible thing.

ROGER: So true. Are you still planning a trip to Seattle? If so, will Freddie accompany you?

ORSON: Yes, I'm going to Seattle in a couple of weeks. I don't need anyone to take care of me; I need someone to keep away the talkative women that subscribe to the concerts. Dealing with these gaggling women is rough going. You know the kind of women who are—

ROGER: Financially comfortable and too important to not be nice to, I suppose.

ORSON: Usually I'm able to avoid such melodrama. I'm uniquely well placed in that I'm not the conductor of the symphony, whose job it is to encourage these ladies to keep giving money. I'm just a visiting guest, and they should be nice to me. I can close the door and say I need to rest. The poor conductor has to go to all the cocktail parties. It's only the very big boys who dare not to turn up for Mrs. McMillan's apple bobbing.

ROGER: When will you begin *Cradle*?

ORSON: I'm doing *Cradle* right after Christmas.

ROGER: It's in production?

ORSON: Yes. I'm going to shoot it in Italy and finish it in New York. I'll be going to New York in about ten days and I was going to try to talk you into coming to New York.

ROGER: You'll only need a day or two in New York won't you?

ORSON: About five days. I'll pick up a couple of actors and choose some locations.

ROGER: Maybe I'll come out for just a day to see you.

ORSON: I wish you would. I'd love it.

ROGER: But you'll be so tied up with—

ORSON: No, I won't. I will be when I come back and start shooting. Then, I'll have a lot of people on salary and I'll have to work all day and then flop into bed.

ROGER: Is there enough of Manhattan left from the '30s for you to use? It's changed so.

ORSON: Yes, there are a few locations that will work. But, much of the pre-Second World War character of New York and Chicago hardly exists anymore. Everybody builds these mirror boxes, and every second front is a front that didn't exist in the '30s. I'm going to do most of the exteriors in New York. I've been to New York many times in the last few years, and I have no sense of coming back to a town where I used to live. There's a little corner here and there, and that's about it. Ah, Roger. I'm going to call you tomorrow because I've got a little deadline here. I've got to get some papers off.

ROGER: I'm so glad to hear from you. Bye.

[Lights dim.]

ACT TWO
SCENE SIX
NOVEMBER 17, 1984
IT'S AN ORWELLIAN KIND OF FABRICATION

Interior of Orson and Roger's libraries. Roger's telephone rings and he answers.

ORSON: Roger?

ROGER: How are you?

ORSON: Fine. I'm calling to ask if a trip to New York is going to be possible for you.

ROGER: When you called, did you get the message that was on my phone?

ORSON: No.

ROGER: It said that I might be away. I had to go to the hospital for a series of tests on my head. Oh God, this is a dull subject, but since my fall, I frequently become dizzy as hell. I'm a little scared.

ORSON: I see, and the travel is tough for you.

ROGER: Yes, unfortunately. If we have to talk about the subject I'll tell you.

ORSON: Yes, I'd like to know.

ROGER: Remember, when I came out to your place? I was worried about my insides. Your doctor ordered a brain scan. He examined my head with ultrasound, or some damn thing and told me, "There's a blockage on one side of your brain which bears watching."

ORSON: Yes, and you were worried that you might be going crazy.

ROGER: [Laughing] Exactly. Well, my doctor has been keeping tabs on the blockage and he's now a little concerned that it's increasing. I'm terribly scared, Orson.

ORSON: Yes, you should be.

ROGER: I probably shouldn't travel in the near future. A recent fall, tripping on a rug, seems to have exacerbated the problem.

ORSON: The fall was not because you were dizzy; it was because of the rug. You're still walking in a stately manner that befits an ageless eighty-nine-year-old.

ROGER: [Laughing] I try valiantly to create that illusion.

ORSON: I'm sure you did fall because of the rug, and fall is what you must not do.

ROGER: You're so right.

ORSON: Every fall is a terrible marker on life's highway.

ROGER: Yes, it is.

ORSON: You can get in just as much trouble in Rockford as you can in New York.

ROGER: Yes, I know. But now, I have to face the truth that I'm eighty-nine years old and that is a helluva lot of years.

ORSON: No, if you've got that kind of trouble and you're going nuts [Laughter], you can't come see me in New York.

ROGER: Not New York now, but I'm going to Los Angeles and see you again.

ORSON: No, you're not. When I go to New York, I'll try to go by way of Chicago and Rockford.

ROGER: That would be so wonderful. Anyway, you're really going ahead with *Cradle* and picking out the locations now?

ORSON: Oh, yes, and signing up actors.

ROGER: Great. Filming *Cradle* ought to be easier on you than taking on *Lear*.

ORSON: I'm doing *Lear* after *Cradle*. The French government is behind it. It looks pretty solid.

ROGER: Wonderful. I heard Amy Irving on the radio earlier this week talking about your film. Did you happen to catch her?

ORSON: No. I don't listen to radio and I wish I did, because there's more good stuff on radio than TV. Television is just bankrupt.

ROGER: I remember your telling me years ago that television was going to be wonderful for sporting events. But, there isn't enough talent to make the medium consistently entertaining. The entertainment, if that's the word for it, is for the most part God-awful. You were so right.

ORSON: My reason was wrong though. There is enough talent, but the programming is in the hands of the networks. In radio, it was always in the hands of the sponsor. Campbell Soup was the boss of my show. But Campbell Soup, if it sponsors a TV program today has no control of the content. It just buys time like an advertiser buys space from a newspaper. The networks determine what will run and when it will air. They invite audiences and hook them up with wires, like they did to you, only instead of seeing whether you're going nuts [laughter], they hook up the wires to see whether you approve of a certain sentence. These shows are increasingly based on bizarre computer-generated findings. It's an Orwellian kind of fabrication, and it's getting worse and worse as the technology for polling the public gets more sophisticated. That's something I didn't foresee. I always thought it would get worse, but I didn't know why.

ROGER: It is a little Orwellian certainly.

ORSON: The vast majority of the programming is geared to satisfy the lowest common denominator. Radio had such a wide spectrum from terrible to wonderful. Television really doesn't. It's an accidental moment that's any good. The public is so grateful for a second rate performance, and consider it wonderful because, most television fare is fifth rate, or worse. Speaking of which, *Scene of the Crime* is about to air. You're going to be seeing me every week. I've done three of them and I'll do the rest abroad. At the beginning, I set the scene. I reappear at the end, and tell a joke or two that ties the thing together. But at least I'm on TV and making a little money from it. I'll send you *Cradle* today.

ROGER: Terrific.

ORSON: Bye.

[Lights dim.]

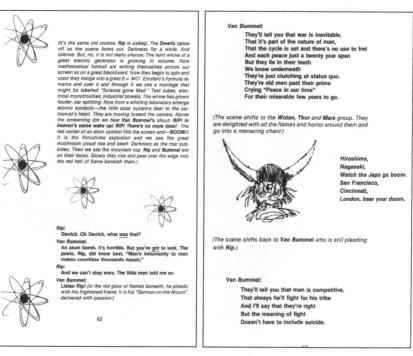

(It's the same old routine. Rip is asleep. The Dwarfs tiptoe off as the scene fades out. Darkness for a while. And silence. But, no, it is not really silence. The faint whine of a great electric generator is growing in volume. Now mathematical formuli are writing themselves across our screen as on a great blackboard. Now they begin to spin and soon they merge into a great $E = MC^2$. Einstein's formula remains and over it and through it we see a montage that might be labelled "Science gone Mad." Test tubes, electrical monstrosities, industrial bowels. The whine has grown louder, ear splitting. Now from a whirling laboratory emerge atomic symbols—the little solar systems dear to the cartoonist's heart. They are moving toward the camera. Above the screaming din we hear **Van Bummel's** shout: RIP! In heaven's name wake up! RIP! There's no more time! The red center of an atom symbol fills the screen and—BOOM!! It is the Hiroshima explosion and we see the great mushroom cloud rise and swell. Darkness as the roar subsides. Then we see the mountain top. Rip and Bummel are on their faces. Slowly they rise and peer over the edge into the red hell of flame beneath them.)

Rip:
Derrick. Oh Derrick, what was that?
Van Bummel:
An atom bomb. It's horrible. But you've got to look. The poets, Rip, did know best. "Man's inhumanity to man makes countless thousands mourn."
Rip:
And we can't stop wars. The little men told me so.
Van Bummel:
Listen Rip! (In the red glow of flames beneath, he pleads with his frightened friend. It is his "Sermon-on-the-Mount" delivered with passion:)

62

Van Bummel:
They'll tell you that war is inevitable,
That it's part of the nature of man,
That the cycle is set and there's no use to fret
And each peace just a twenty year span
But they lie in their teeth
We know underneath
They're just clutching at status quo.
They're old men past their prime
Crying "Peace in our time"
For their miserable few years to go.

(The scene shifts to the **Wotan, Thor** and **Mars** group. They are delighted with all the flames and horror around them and go into a menacing chant:)

Hiroshima,
Nagasaki,
Watch the Japs go boom.
San Francisco,
Cincinnati,
London, hear your doom.

(The scene shifts back to **Van Bummel** who is still pleading with Rip.)

Van Bummel:
They'll tell you that man is competitive,
That always he'll fight for his tribe
And I'll say that they're right
But the meaning of fight
Doesn't have to include suicide.

The final four pages from the *Rip Van Winkle Renascent* screenplay.

(The Puppets continue their chant:)

*Hiroshima
Nagasaki
Bummel thinks some bars
Will hold us in
He's full of gin,
We're Wotan, Thor and Mars.*

*Van Bummel:
If you happen to come from Texas
You'll be proud of that lone star state
But you'll save some zeal
For the commonweal
Of our Nation—God keep her great.
And while you can love your country
And boast you're American
You can still hold allegience to a world
And make it an Eden for Man.*

*Mars etc.
Hiroshima! Nagasaki!
Wotan, Thor and Mars.
Forget your qualms,
With atom bombs
Now we can crack the stars!*

*(During this final chant, **Rip** has risen in righteous wrath.
He strides over to **Mars** and with one great blow strikes him
down. The camera is now out in space and from there we
can see the evil spirits tumbling down, down, down. In
their fall they miss the Earth entirely and continue on into
outer darkness. Now **Rip** opens the **Bummel** book and
reads aloud the final verses:)*

64

Rip:
**Then the war-drums beat no longer and the battle flags were furled
In the Parliment of Man, the Federation of the World.**

**There the common sense of most did hold a fretful world in awe
And the kindly earth did prosper lapped in universal law.**

*At long last, **Rip** is standing erect. Inspired. He looks up and
sees the Tennyson prophesy written bold across a blue sky,*

Now three titles appear:

In the original story. Rip
only nodded off long enough
to miss the American Revolution.
We kept him up there in the
mountains right down to the
nuclear age.

The makers of this film,
members of the Todd School,
have bombarded him with the
great issue of Life and Death
on this planet and hereby
apologize for not including
any final solution.

65

ACT TWO
SCENE SEVEN
DECEMBER 7, 1984
DEVOTION IS HARD TO FIND

Interior of Orson and Roger's libraries. Roger's telephone rings.

ROGER: [Voice Message: This is Roger Hill. Leave a message after the beep.]

ORSON: Roger, sorry I missed you. I'll call you later.

ROGER: Hello, Orson?

ORSON: Oh, hello. You never answer your phone. Forever the man of mystery.

ROGER: When I don't pick up the phone, it doesn't mean I'm gone. All you have to do is say, "Orson calling," and I'll call you back. I don't want to pick up the phone for everyone.

ORSON: You're just hiding. I do the same thing.

ROGER: So, what's happening? Are you going to leave for New York shortly?

ORSON: Soon, yes.

ROGER: But you haven't set a date?

ORSON: No. I'm at the mercy of elements other than my own. But, it will be very soon. I'm just calling to chat. No particular messages.

ROGER: That's fine, except—

ORSON: Except you have to go somewhere?

ROGER: Except that you were going to send me a script, damn it.

ORSON: I did! I wrote it out on the envelope myself. I'll find out if Freddie forgot to mail it. I'll check with him today.

ROGER: There's no hurry, but be sure before you go away you send me a copy.

ORSON: I did. Freddie may not have sent it, he's an eccentric.

ROGER: [Laughs] Aren't we all?

ORSON: He's a sort of a tall Shorty [George "Shorty" Chirello] [Laughing]. I'm very grateful to him. He's cheerful and he's devoted.

ROGER: Oh, yes, and that's worth a great deal.

ORSON: You bet. Devotion is hard to find. I'm taking your advice and bringing him to Europe with me. I don't know whether he'll be able to stand it though. Being Italian he has to talk, and he doesn't speak Italian.

ROGER: You think he may be at a bit of a loss in Italy?

ORSON: Like most Italian-Americans, who visit their native land for the first time, he may be lost initially. Most of the immigrants are from the south, which is quite distinct culturally from the rest of the country. When their descendants return and venture north, they enter a new and often confounding culture. By the time transplanted Italians have acculturated here for a generation or two, like Freddie, their native tongue gets pretty tattered. The Italians have about ten major dialects that are almost separate languages, which adds to the challenge of returning Italians. Different words and each dialect is quite distinctive.

ROGER: What kind of Italian do you speak?

ORSON: I speak the bad version of the accepted modern Italian, which I don't like. It's not as good as Tuscan Italian, but it's what the Romans taught everybody, and is spoken on radio and television. The Florentine language is much more beautiful, but I don't aspire to that, never. I surrendered to speak a basic Roman Italian, which is similar to the English the BBC taught everybody in England to speak over the air. The same is true here. Americans have flattened out the English language. Most regional differences have vanished. There is a Texas accent that everybody in that part of the country speaks, the Southern voice is distinct, and a Yankee voice remains in portions of New England. That's about all that's left. You can tell an Okie, you can tell a Louisianan, and you can tell a Carolinian. Those are different enough, and, of course, a Boston accent is easy. But telling the difference between somebody from Ohio, Wisconsin, or Illinois is far more problematic.

ROGER: It would be tough.

ORSON: I don't hear the differences. But, I'm no longer in the business of trying to speak different dialects like I used to when I was in radio. My ear is not as attuned as it once was. I think TV is a great leveler of everything, the great flattener. [Laughter] It has

"She complicates and renders my life more expensive every day. But, I must keep her close because she's just a little thing that depends so totally on me."

contributed considerably to our disturbingly homogenized culture. I'm sure that were I in Rockford, aside from size, I would see very little difference from Los Angeles except the weather.

ROGER: I'm relieved to hear that you're taking Freddie with you to Italy.

ORSON: Then I have to take my poodle, Kiki, too.

ROGER: Oh, that malevolent black beast—

ORSON: I just can't abandon her.

ROGER: That's right.

ORSON: She complicates and renders my life more expensive every day. But, I must keep her close because she's just a little thing that depends so totally on me.

ROGER: Are there restaurants in Europe that allow her to accompany you?

ORSON: Oh, yes. Throughout Europe, restaurants welcome you and your dog. America and England, the two Anglo-Saxon countries, dog-loving countries, are the only places that don't allow dogs.

ROGER: You mean England won't let them in either?

ORSON: Oh, no. If you try, you are greeted with, "Oh, no, no, no. Certainly not, sir, we don't cater to canines." But in France, you can bring a Great Dane to the fanciest restaurant and you both will receive equal pampering. The same is true in Italy. It's very strange that the freethinking world is tough about taking dogs in restaurants. There is a French restaurant here in Hollywood where I go, and, although it's against the laws of California, they let me take my little poodle, who bites the waiters.

ROGER: That's right, Ma Maison. But they also let you in Chasen's when we dined there not long ago.

ORSON: Yes. There are two or three places where I have that license. But if I weren't a kind of a tattered, second-rate celebrity, I wouldn't have a chance.

ROGER: There's a possibility that you'll find Britain has changed.

ORSON: Oh, no! I've been there recently. You forget, I was there this spring.

ROGER: What about Britain's attitude toward admitting women to their clubs? My Cliff Dwellers membership has reciprocal rights with several clubs in London. Several years ago, when Horty and I were visiting friends in London, we suggested taking them to the Savage Club. They were thrilled. We got as far as the front steps. When the doorman saw Horty and two other women in our party, he shrieked, "Oh, no, no, no women!"

ORSON: Allowed in the club?

ROGER: Exactly. However, I understand now that, in the afternoon, even in London, many clubs tolerate women in their midst.

ORSON: They're allowed in some clubs, not all, not the really grand ones. Allowing women is regarded as a thin-edged wedge. [Laughter] Before the war, there were no women at all in the clubs. Waiters served your food. But now, they're reduced to enduring waitresses. It is pretty silly that you can't bring your wife, but the whole point of the English club is to get away from the women.

ROGER: Well, life has its inconsistencies.

ORSON: I've never belonged to any club. But I've been a guest in the very grand English ones. My God, you're afraid to take a step for fear of doing something wrong. [Laughter] I tried to join the Players Club years ago, when I was a young sprig, but I was blackballed.

ROGER: Really?

ORSON: Yes, and I found out it was for rowdyism.
            [Uproarious laughter] The Cliff Dwellers reminds
            me of a book I read the other day. It's set in
            Chicago at the time I was going to Todd. It
            brought to the surface places I haven't thought of
            in decades, the Cliff Dwellers, Henrici's, and
            Thompson's. We used to eat at Thompson's.

ROGER: Thompson's?

ORSON: Yes, it was a kind of a Horn & Hardart, which was
            in New York, made famous for its coin-operated
            Automats. Thompson's was more of a cafeteria.

ROGER: Yes, and you ate off the arm of a chair, didn't
            you?

ORSON: Yes. They had a Kroch's bookstore nearby, I
            remember.

ROGER: Yes.

ORSON: I haven't been to Chicago in a million years.
            Remember, Oscar Wilde, the "Apostle of
            Aestheticism," as he was billed on his 1882 tour of
            America, was barred from Chicago society when on
            a stop in the city he referred to the Water Tower as
            a "monstrosity with pepper boxes stuck all over it."
            [Laughter] That *bon mot* closed a lot of doors to
            him. I read that in *Oscar Wilde Discovers America*,
            a book about the tour, co-written by the nice
            fellow who wrote the book about Lincoln's
            assassination, and another tome on Sherman,
            Lloyd Lewis. His book on Wilde is delightful. The
            D'Oyly Carte Opera Company sent Wilde on this
            tour of America. Gilbert and Sullivan had written
            the operetta, *Patience*, which was making fun of
            Oscar Wilde. The D'Oyly Carte Opera Company,

which put on the play, knew that the American public wouldn't get the joke, and, for that reason, they sent Wilde ahead to lecture, so that everybody would be aware of him and his connection to the operetta.

ROGER: D'Oyly Carte Opera Company, that's the Gilbert and Sullivan outfit.

ORSON: Yes, they were the people who owned the operettas, and, with the profits, they built the Savoy Hotel. [Doorbell rings.] I need to push a button and see that somebody gets in, and get to work.

ROGER: Bye.

[Lights dim.]

ACT TWO
SCENE EIGHT
DECEMBER 11, 1984
HOW DO YOU ENDURE THESE BLOWS?

Interior of Orson and Roger's libraries. Roger's telephone rings.

ORSON: Roger. Hi.

ROGER: I was just going to call you. I finished your script. Jesus God, that's going to be wonderful. I think it's going to make headlines, particularly the last touch with Virginia.

ORSON: You like it, huh?

ROGER: Oh God, that's a beautiful ending, the counter-point between all the excitement inside and your little personal problems out there. It's a stunning thing.

ORSON: Oh, I'm delighted.

ROGER: It's wonderful. And they're going to hear all over the country that last line. What the hell is it— [Laughter] Virginia says, "I don't like that joke about divorce," and you respond, "You started it. And it isn't really a joke. A movie actor—a divorced movie actor—as president? Not a chance."

ORSON: Well, yesterday I got the word that we don't have the money for it.

ROGER: Oh, for—No kidding?

ORSON: Yup. The production schedule was set, sets were built, much of the casting was completed, and we were three weeks away from shooting exteriors in Hoboken and Staten Island.

ROGER: How do you endure these blows?

ORSON: It is just terrible news. The sky fell in about six o'clock last night. The only positive glimmer is that I own the script and all the actors are crazy to do it. Everybody in Hollywood who has read it wants to do it. It's not a project that nobody wants to touch.

ROGER: It's so beautifully done. The way the ending builds is extraordinary. The young couple outside and all the screaming inside. It's a surefire thing.

ORSON: I have a wonderful cast. I have everything. Except the money. I own the production and the script.

ROGER: You're not tied up with the producer? He doesn't own you?

ORSON: No. I never signed a thing.

ROGER: Then, it's just a matter of finding the money from another source?

ORSON: Yes. But, that's not always easy. In this case, it's easier than usual because there's an enormous interest in it.

ROGER: I would think so. Much of the public has forgotten all about *Cradle*, but everybody in the business knows the story.

ORSON: No, they don't know the story. They just like the script and the cast. Most of them are too young to know what the hell it's all about. Producers are all under forty. They used to be under seventy. But they seem to like it very much, and, as I say, there's a lot of excitement about it. But, it was quite a belly flop because I planned in a week to start shooting.

ROGER: I'm sorry Hortense isn't alive to see your script because we were so tied up with you that summer.

ORSON: I know. What I have written is not strictly factual, but it is essentially the truth.

ROGER: It really is. It's essentially the truth about you and Virginia.

ORSON: I'm very frank about myself.

ROGER: Exactly. Yes, you can see and feel your spirit of youthfulness. I think it's wonderful. Nobody could have done as good a job.

ORSON: It was difficult to do. Very difficult to distance myself from myself, to be objective.

ROGER: You have captured a unique and a little cock-eyed time when you were just out of your teens and in charge of everything.

ORSON: And the not-quite-grown-up quality of it, I think, is very good. I'm very proud of it. I think it's the best thing I've ever written.

ROGER: Quit talking to an admirer and find some money for God's sakes.

ORSON: Oh, yes. I have to be very careful. It's a delicate walk on eggshells, but I think there's hope. Thank God, none of the actors were under contract with the producer. They're free to follow me. But, if I don't arrange financing soon, I will lose them.

ROGER: You mean to say that he hasn't got a signature of any one of your cast?

ORSON: Not one. You remember that old joke of Jack Warner's quoting Sam Goldwyn?

ROGER: No.

ORSON: He said, "A verbal commitment with someone is not worth the paper it's written on." [Laughter] That's what it is. I kept asking for five months to have a contract and, thank God, I didn't get it. In the contract he sent me, he had cut my salary by $300,000.

ROGER: Well, that probably kept you from signing it. It sounds terribly Byzantine.

ORSON: Funding a film oftentimes is. It's taken me a hundred and ten years to learn the technical and legal nuances necessary to finance a movie. The great legend about me is that I have a psychotic fear of finishing a picture, and my argument is that I have a psychotic fear of not beginning a picture. [Laughter]

ROGER: Well, get at it, Orson. I'm elated and, yet now, I'm scared as hell.

ORSON: Stay elated. I just wanted to hear what you thought of the script.

ROGER: [Laughing] I loved it and I love you.

ORSON: Oh, God bless you. Talk to you soon. Bye.

ROGER: Bye.

[Lights dim.]

CURTAIN

There exists a real treasury of PHOTOGRAPHS recording the desolation, anguish and the curious beauty of Americans standing up straight in the midst of that long storm we remember as the years of our Great Depression . . . The MAIN TITLES . . . and the visual background of most of the OPENING NARRATION will feature a significant selection of these photos.

SERIES OF SHOTS: NEW YORK STREETS—NIGHT

ORSON WELLES'S VOICE

This happened (and it really did happen) in the midst of the Great Depression. Franklin Roosevelt was President and one third of the nation was ill housed, ill clad, and ill nourished. He said that. And he was right. But misery seemed to draw us together. There never was a time when people were so nice to each other. Even a tough town like New York was like a friendly little village. Here comes Mrs. J. Sargeant Cram (who really existed) cruising the streets in her Rolls-Royce . . .

The headlights of the limousine pick out some wretched people trying to sleep on the pavement. A cruel wind is blowing. (The action is as Orson Welles describes it.)

When she sees some homeless person crouched on the sidewalks (and they're easy to find) she stops and sends out her footman with a stone— (the Rolls is full of stones). Close to each person the footman leaves a wad of wet money, and places a stone on it so the wind won't blow it away . . . We'll learn a little later why the money happens to be wet . . .

By now the footman (with the chauffeur to help) has finished doling out money to this particular band of derelicts. The car is about to start.

MRS. CRAM
(whose dignity is simple and authentic even if
she does look like George Washington in drag)
Stop. Do you hear that, Jason?—a peculiar noise?

JASON
No, Mrs. Cram.

MRS. CRAM
I do: it sounds like a horse dancing. That wouldn't be likely, would it, Jason?

JASON
No, Ma'am, not likely at all.

The first page of Orson's *The Cradle Will Rock* screenplay.

HARRY'S VOICE: Arrest them!

MARTY: Arrest them? There's thousands of 'em!

WILL: My God! What do they want with me?

CUT BACK TO:

127. EXTERIOR. THE STREET OUTSIDE THE SEVILLE THEATRE—
NIGHT

VIRGINIA and ORSON, still on their slow stroll, are now on their way back to the fire exit. ("The Cradle" can be heard within)—

VIRGINIA

So how about it? . . .

ORSON

About what?

VIRGINIA

You really think it's time to make your big change in careers? After tonight you've got this town in the palm of your hand.

ORSON

Good time to quit . . .

VIRGINIA

Aren't you just a little tempted by Hollywood?

ORSON

Hollywood is a place where you must never sit down because when you stand up you're sixty-five years old.
(smiling)
No, you'll simply have to make up your mind about that divorce.

They stop and turn to each other.

VIRGINIA

That or Washington . . . ? Will I have to kiss a lot of strange babies?

ORSON

That's me. You just have to be gracious.

VIRGINIA
(after a beat)
I don't like that joke about divorce.

ORSON

You started it. And it isn't really a joke . . .
(beat)
A movie actor—a *divorced* movie actor—as president—? Not a chance.

The penultimate page of Orson's *The Cradle Will Rock* screenplay

ACT THREE
SCENE ONE
MARCH 20, 1985
EVERY GREAT CAREER IS A ROLLER COASTER

*Interior of Orson and Roger's libraries. Roger's telephone rings and he
answers.*

ORSON: Roger. How are you?

ROGER: I'm wonderful. My doctor tells me I'm well enough
to travel.

ORSON: Great. Now that spring is in the air, can I convince
you to fly out to California or Las Vegas for an
extended visit?

ROGER: I'm very tempted. Let me check my calendar and
get back to you with possible dates. I always keep
thinking there's one chance in a thousand that you
will to fly to your Midwest once more. Don't you
have any nostalgia in your bones?

ORSON: None at all. There are so many places in the world
I have nostalgia for, considering how many places
I've been over a long life, and every one of them
has been horribly changed. I don't want to see that
change. I don't want to see Woodstock as a suburb
of Chicago. What pleasure would that give me?
Chicago would be different. I'd kind of like to
see Chicago.

ROGER: I'd like to sit once more with you in the number one booth in the restaurant at the Ambassador.

ORSON: Oh, yes, I'd love it. But, again, it would be sad. It's no longer one of the glamorous places of the world. It's just another hotel owned by a chain. I don't travel except for a job because I hate to see the modern world coming between me and my memories. Paris, London, and New York are just not the same cities. But I'll meet you on neutral territory, if that's the condition to shorten your trip and bring us together, I'll travel to Greece or anywhere you suggest.

ROGER: Perhaps in a few months, I can fly out to Hollywood. But, my mind now is on your childhood. Did you receive the photograph I sent of your father's old hotel in Grand Detour?

ORSON: Oh, yes. That photograph was taken before my father died. I remember the addition he built and the photograph predates those changes.

ROGER: He made changes?

ORSON: Yes. I was never in the hotel until my father altered the place. He rented a home in Grand Detour and we lived there for a year before he bought the hotel. I remember the house vividly. The hotel my father bought, I remember with equal clarity. He bought it, a general store, and a lot of farmland from an old guy by the name of Sheffield.

ROGER: Wasn't there some thought that Sheffield or your father set fire to the place because it was highly insured?

ORSON: No. [Ruefully laughing] No, my father was drunk
              when the place when up in smoke. There was no
              crookedness in that. I never knew the place was
              highly insured.

ROGER: Oh, really? According to the story some of the old
              timers in Grand Detour tell, there was a great
              insurance policy on the place.

ORSON: There might have been, but I think my father
              cared a great deal about the hotel. He housed his
              jade collection there, which was lost in the fire.
              He had never thought of insuring it.

ROGER: Let me ask you a question. As you come into
              Grand Detour, there's an historical sign, which has
              a paragraph or two about the community being the
              home of John Deere and his plow. Well, I think
              there also ought to be a little notice of the hotel
              that burned down, which was quite an historic
              spot, and the Orson Welles mention. I'm reasonably
              certain the village would do this if I approached
              the city fathers.

ORSON: Oh for—Why? We're all going to be dumped
              eventually. What does Mann say on the subject?
              "*Hold fast the time! Guard it, watch over it, every
              hour, every minute! Unregarded it slips away like a
              lizard, smooth, slippery, faithless. Hold every
              moment sacred. Give each clarity and meaning,
              each the weight of thine awareness, each its true
              and due fulfillment.*" [Laughs ruefully] I don't
              think I did anything of note in Grand Detour
              and that's why I think it would be pompous to
              introduce myself. After all, the entire territory
              is now given over as sacred ground to Ronnie
              Reagan.

ROGER: I accept your argument. On the other hand, unless you haven't definitely ruled me out, I'm going to broach the subject with the good burghers of your long ago haunts.

ORSON: Oh, I don't forbid it. But permit me to giggle quietly and think how much happier I'd be if you'd use the time to visit your old lonely friend because the only real existence we have is the people we love. Putting up little signposts and putting notices in libraries where the paper will rot away in seventy years is inexpedient. I don't believe in terrestrial immortality. I have my doubts about the other, but I'm damn sure that terrestrial immortality is a fickle lady at best.

ROGER: Have you begun your memoir?

ORSON: Yes. I've begun writing a few personal sketches. I'm currently cobbling together a few reminiscences on staging *Macbeth* in Harlem.

ROGER: Wonderful.

ORSON: Yes, I practically lived in Harlem for a time because I had a reason to be there and I was very young, and wasn't made to feel a stranger. After all, it was at the end of the great golden age of Harlem when there was a big international colony of people like Nancy Cunard and other grand folks who lived there. So, there was still this feeling among the Blacks that, if Honky was smart enough, he would see where the life was really great. Every second door was a soul food restaurant and next door to that was a Metcalf or an Emperor of Ethiopia or something. Father Divine was a great force as well. The WPA represented a real chance for thousands of people to stay alive. We had everybody from gangsters to just ordinary folks engaged in the arts. It was a great experience. You got to know the denizens of Harlem on a level that you wouldn't as an employer or an anthropologist. I remember one night, I was exhausted from my over-extended hours. I had to pick from a group of actors somebody to do double duty to construct sets, and I started saying, "Eenie, Meenie, Minie, Mo." [Laughter] I thought I was going to have to take the "A Train." Oh, but it was a unique experience.

ROGER: Of course, it was.

ORSON: When rehearsing in those days, I didn't require any sleep at all. I used to support myself as a radio actor before I had my own show. We could only rehearse *Macbeth*, which we rehearsed a long time because the actors had never read Shakespeare, from twelve midnight on because the theatre was needed during the day for other rehearsals and for performances in the evening. So, rehearsals started at midnight and ended about five. At the close of rehearsals, I'd walk to a block party or go to Black-only nightclubs and sit around for an hour or two. Then, I would walk home through Central Park and watch the sun come up. There was never a thought of danger. I'm scared inside a locked car now. It's terrible to see the change.

ROGER: There's a book to write just on your days in Harlem.

ORSON: It was a very strange and wonderful affair, staging *Macbeth* at the Lafayette Theatre. Before it opened, we experienced tremendous anger for putting on the play. Once I was saved from being cut on my face with razors. There was considerable feeling, worked up by the Communists that we were going to do an Uncle Tom act. By opening night, the traffic was blocked for five blocks around the theatre, with people screaming for it and against it. It was a caldron boiling with excitement and rage. When the play was over, there were so many curtain calls that, at the end, they kept the curtain up and the people in the audience came on the stage with the actors. I'd never seen that before. It was very thrilling. It ran for ten sold-out weeks before moving downtown to the Adelphi Theatre.

ROGER: The reviews were sensational. Brooks Atkinson at the *Times* raved as did a host of others. Well, not all the critics. Who was the fellow that panned the production with such vitriol that one of the performers put a hex on him?

ORSON: Percy Hammond of the anti-New Deal *Herald Tribune*. An African drummer with diamond studded gold teeth, known as Jazzbo, one of several drummers who backed up the wailing voodoo witches, asked me, "You want we make beri-beri on this bad man?" I told him to make all the beri-beri he desired. He fashioned a voodoo doll to represent Hammond, stuck the miniature effigy with pins, and put a death curse on him. Within twenty-four hours, the "bad man" would be dead, Jazzbo assured me. He was overly optimistic. Hammond survived the next day, but Jazzbo was convinced that it was his beri-beri that felled Hammond several days later. [Laughter.]

ROGER: What a story. Your mentioning the communists in New York brings back other memories. At least two or three times, we were in New York on May Day.

ORSON: Oh yes, the great parade and everything. Those were the days of the popular front. The Communists' agitation and infiltration of Harlem was very notable. What headaches the party gave us back then. If I had ever been asked to name Communists and I had wanted to, I could have pointed fingers for two days. They never called me. I kept asking to be called. I begged to be called because I wanted to describe the difference between the progressives or liberals and the Communists. They didn't want that. That got me out of it because I was on every list in the world. I was the head of the committee to defend Harry Bridges. [Laughter.]

ROGER: What days they were. I had parents come to me who had read that my cousin, Edwin Embree, head of the Rosenwald Foundation and head of Todd's board, was suspect, and I was a bit jealous.

ORSON: He was suspect and you weren't [laughter].

ROGER: Yes, but a bit later, I was delighted when another parent said he'd read somewhere that Roger Hill was being looked at because of some "left" teachers he was hiring. I was very proud of that report.

ORSON: I know just what you mean. I told you what happened to me in Ireland?

ROGER: No.

ORSON: One day in the late '40s, not long after the war, Hilton Edwards called me up and said that he and Micheál mac Liammóir had a play that some producers wanted to bring to London. He wanted my advice as to whether it would be a success there. I hadn't been back in Ireland for 2,000 years, so I was happy to return to Dublin. I thought it would be wonderful to see all my old friends. I arrived at about five in the afternoon, met by about twenty policemen, and was informed by one of them, "We're going to be guarding you." I said "What from?" And the officer responded, "Well, from the demonstrators." Some group called the Bleeding Heart of Jesus or something, had organized a rally of people who were opposed to my coming. [Laughter]. They had about two thousand people with placards reading, "Go Back To Moscow, Stalin Star," which they flailed in my face. During the play, you could hear this crowd outside sounding like very enthusiastic actors in a spirited melodrama about the French revolution. The crowd was protesting my earlier appearance at an American-Soviet Friendship Rally at Madison Square Garden. The chairman was Mrs. Roosevelt, and I was in a group of well-known Communists, which included Omar Bradley and General Eisenhower. [Uproarious laughter]. "Go Back to Moscow, Stalin Star," the crowd chanted. I hope such madness doesn't come again, but it's hard to be hopeful.

ROGER: God, let's hope not.

ORSON: All right. Let us return to a subject on which you are very evasive. How about a little trip to see me?

ROGER: I won't be evasive. Eventually, I'll get out there, but it won't be for a while.

ORSON: I hope before it's time to give the eulogy at my funeral.

ROGER: [Laughs] That's right. I hope to hell that's not the one thing that brings you here. If there's anything I'm trying to avoid, it's a funeral.

ORSON: I rather seriously refused to go to my friends' funerals when I was younger. Now, I'm often asked

to offer the eulogy. I think that if I'm asked, I
should oblige. So, I've seen a lot of coffins in
recent years—Arnold Weissberger, George Schaefer,
Hans Conried—

ROGER: Dwight Whitney, who was a few years behind you
            at Todd—

ORSON: Yes, for years he was the head of *TV Guide's*
            Hollywood bureau, we keep in touch.

ROGER: He sent me your Darryl Zanuck eulogy a couple of
            years ago.

ORSON: Darryl died five Decembers ago. What a towering
            Gulliver among Lilliputians he was.

[Scrim: Sixty-four-year-old Orson reading his Zanuck eulogy]

At Winston Churchill's funeral, there was a moment when the coffin
was to be carried out of Westminster Abbey and onto a barge for a
trip up the Thames River. A special group of pallbearers from the
various military services in Great Britain was selected for this. One, a
sailor, broke his ankle carrying the coffin down the stone steps of
the Abbey. For a moment it seemed that the coffin would drop to
the ground, but it was safely carried onto the barge.

Afterward officials said to the sailor, 'How did you manage to go
on?'

And the sailor said, 'I would have carried him all over London.'

That's the way I feel about my friend Darryl Zanuck. Churchill wrote
the script for his own funeral. Lord Mountbatten recently did the
same thing in England—in England, if you're going to have a state
funeral, they let you do that. They give you what amounts to a
final cut. We don't have state funerals in our movie community,

but if we did, Darryl would certainly have been given one—and he would have produced it. And what a show that would have been. Virginia and Dick have reminded me that Darryl himself would not wish this occasion to be too lugubrious. That's true. I'm pretty sure that if he were the producer in charge of this occasion, Darryl would have wished for us all to leave this gathering with lightened spirits. The trouble is that I'm the wrong man for that job—I can't find anything cheerful to say about the loss of my friend. To understand the special nature of his contributions, we must understand the full meaning of the word producer in Darryl's day. In the Golden Age of Hollywood, it meant something quite different than it does now. There were producers assigned to each movie, and then there was the man in charge of all the movies. In Darryl's day that was a lot of movies, forty, fifty, sixty, seventy feature pictures a year. He was one of the legendary tycoons presiding over productions.

The whole point about Darryl was that he did not just preside. He did so very much more than preside. Of all the big-boss producers, Darryl was unquestionably the man with the greatest gifts—true personal, professional, and artistic gifts for the filmmaking process itself. He began as a writer and in a sense he never stopped functioning as a writer. Others may have matched him as a star-maker, but with all of Darryl's flair for the magic personalities, his first commitment was always to the story. For Darryl that was what it was to make a film: to tell a story.

God bless him for that. With half a hundred and more stories to tell every dozen months, this great storyteller was, of necessity, an editor and a great editor. There never was an editor in our business to touch him.

Every great career is a roller coaster and Darryl's had his disasters. He knew eclipse. He knew comebacks and triumphs. And then there were studio politics, and that's the roughest game there is. But has anybody—anybody—ever claimed that Darryl Zanuck advanced himself by dirty tricks? Or by leaving behind him the usual trail of bloody corpses? Of course, there were some aching egos and some bruised temperaments. If you're in charge of a regiment of artists, some of your commands are going to hurt. Some of your decisions are bound to seem arbitrary, but Darryl didn't sign on to be a recreation director of a summer camp. Of course, he was tough. That was his job. But unlike many of the others, he was never cruel. Never vindictive. He wasn't, and what a rare thing it is to say in the competitive game of ours, he was a man totally devoid of malice. But he was great with irony. Great sense of humor, even about himself; of which of the others can we say that?

I always knew that if I did something really outrageous, that if I committed some abominable crime, and if all the police in the world were after me, there was one man, and only one man I could come to, and that was Darryl. He would not have made a speech about the good of the industry or the good of his studio. He would not have been mealy-mouthed or put me aside. He would have hid me under the bed. Very simply, he was a friend. I don't mean just my friend. I mean that friendship was something he was very good at.

And that is why it is so very hard to say good-bye to him.

[Lights dim.]

ROGER: There are too many good-byes in old age.

ORSON: And too few hellos.

ROGER: So, I won't say good-bye. Instead, be of good cheer.

ORSON: A toast to good cheer and to you.

[Lights dim.]

Orson and his dog Caesar.

"I've never felt particularly sentimental about the Fourth of July except when I was younger than you ever knew me. When I was in Grand Detour, I used to see the old Gray and Blue guys marching along."

ACT THREE
SCENE TWO
MAY 6, 1985
I COME WITH A CALL TO ACTION

Interior of Orson and Roger's libraries. Orson's telephone rings.

ORSON: [Recorded message] Please leave a message. Orson.

ROGER: Orson, sorry I missed you. Happy birthday. I hold
in my hand a copy of a letter I wrote you twenty
years ago, in which I reminded you of my approaching
seventieth birthday, and which, I predicted, would
likely be my year of Finality, the year I reached
three score and ten, the inevitable diminution of
life's earlier abundance. Foolish superstition, you
wrote back. Hortense shared your sneers. And all
the family pointed to Noble Hill, who flourished
for almost a century. A biblical boyhood, however,
couldn't be erased. It is written in the Psalms. So, I
told myself, it must be written in the stars. Twenty
years ago, I convinced myself that each unforgiving
annum must be crammed with 52 weeks' worth
of distance run. I outran the *Bible* and I've been
running on borrowed time ever since. I've beaten
the Psalmists by almost twenty years. As I approach
ninety, I wonder if beating the odds is a miracle or
a curse. In the yellowed carbon, I wrote that you,
too, had entered a biblical year of great importance:
the year of the jubilee. You will remember the
Leviticus origin of this celebration: seven is, of

course, the charmed number throughout Hebrew culture. Every seventh year must be a sabbatical one. During this time, even the land must rest by lying fallow. Then, at the seventh sabbatical, comes the climax of all: the great 49th year of the jubilee. This was the year for the manumission of slaves, the freeing of prisoners, the singing of Hosannas to God for his mercies. Now, you have arrived at three score and ten. May you outrun Psalmists for many years to come, too. With abiding love.

[Lights dim.]

Interior of Orson and Roger's libraries, May 11, 1985. Roger's telephone rings.

ROGER: Hello.

ORSON: Roger. What are you up to?

ROGER: Sword fighting with the Grim Reaper and keeping him at bay. Speaking of grim, I'm disheartened that news and analysis on television is so baleful, and it brings to mind something else I think you should do in addition to your movie projects and magic show.

ORSON: Tell me something else I should be doing.

ROGER: Raising the standard of news broadcasting.

ORSON: What would you suggest?

ROGER: The country would be well served if you brought back to television or radio an expanded version of your fifteen-minute *Almanac* program that ran in the mid-'40s.

ORSON: The Lear Radio people gave me a free hand to say anything I wanted, until I started appearing controversial. It was okay to discuss bullfighting and touch ever so lightly on politics, but when I began commenting on our nuclear testing on the Bikini Atoll and other sobering topics of the day, Lear withdrew its sponsorship.

ROGER: Your finest hour, actually many hours, on your *Almanac* was championing a black soldier who, returning to his hometown somewhere in the South, was beaten by a mob. What was his name?

ORSON: Isaac Woodard. He wasn't beaten by a mob, but by a policeman. Woodard was on a bus, not too far from his home in South Carolina. At a stop, he took too much time in the "colored" men's room to satisfy the bus driver. A heated exchange followed, prompting the bus driver to call a cop, who, without provocation, beat the bejesus out of Woodard with a billy club, which blinded him. I immediately inveighed against this mindless madness, and, over the next several months, as the case unfolded, I continued to seethe over the air.

ROGER: Didn't the NAACP contact you?

ORSON: Yes, the NAACP brought Woodard's plight to my attention.

ROGER: Now it comes back. Wasn't he a decorated war hero?

ORSON: He served overseas for over a year and was decorated with a battle star.

[Scrim: Thirty-one-year-old Orson in an ABC radio studio reading his July 28, 1946 commentary.]

Wash your hands, Officer X. Wash them well. Scrub and scour. We will blast out your name. We'll give the world your given name, Officer X. Yes, and your so-called Christian name. Officer X— after I have found you out, I'll never lose you. If they try you, I'm going to watch the trial. If they jail you, I'm going to wait for your first day of freedom. You won't be free of me… You can't get rid of me… Who am I? A masked avenger from the comic books? No, sir. Merely an inquisitive citizen of America.

[Lights dim.]

ORSON: Week after week, I updated my audience on the progress of the case. I was threatened with lawsuits if I didn't cease and desist. The threats only heightened my resolve to make America aware of the bitter fruits of this man's service to his country. A lot of people from the South and North wrote and asked what business was it of mine to involve myself in this case.

[Scrim: Thirty-one-year-old Orson at the ABC microphone reading his Woodard script.]

God judge me if it isn't the most pressing business I have. The blind soldier fought for me in this war. The least I can do now is fight for him. I have eyes. He hasn't. I have a voice on the radio. He hasn't. I was born a white man and until a colored man is a full citizen like me I haven't the leisure to enjoy the freedom that this colored man risked his life for to maintain for me. I don't own what I have until he owns an equal share of it. Until someone beats me, and blinds me, I am in his debt. And so I come to this microphone not as a radio dramatist (although it pays better), not as a commentator (although it's safer to be simply that). I come, in that boy's name, and in the name of all who in this land of ours have no voice of their own. I come with a call to action.

[Lights dim.]

ROGER: What became of the case?

ORSON: The Department of Justice filed charges against the rogue cop.

ROGER: Didn't the NAACP credit you as the prime mover in causing the Government to act?

ORSON: There were a number of us on the side of the angels. I was just the one with a microphone and a weekly national audience. Our broadcasts led to a benefit in New York on Woodard's behalf. Billie Holiday, Milton Berle, Cab Calloway, and many others joined me on stage and performed for an impassioned audience of over 30,000, demanding justice for one black man and for all of black America.

ROGER: Was justice served?

ORSON: Sadly, no. Though the Department of Justice took the case to trial, after fifteen minutes of deliberation, an all-white jury acquitted the cop. I'll never forget a line from the defense attorney's closing argument to the jury, "If you rule against my client, then let South Carolina secede again."

ROGER: Well, it's time for a new *Welles Almanac*.

ORSON: I have a chance to do it, but I can't afford to accept because that man who has an all-news network, [Ted] Turner, will give me anything, except money.

Isaac Woodard is welcomed into The Blinded Veterans Association by acting director Lloyd Greenwood.

He can't pay a salary. His resources are stretched, I'm informed. Apparently he's an old-fashioned Captain Bligh kind of fellow. He's one of those nuts that have whirled loose from the great American machinery of capitalism and are clanking around on their own. It was good hearing your voice.

ROGER: Thanks for calling.

[Lights dim.]

ACT THREE
SCENE THREE
MAY 25, 1985
"WHEN SORROW COME, THEY COME
NOT SINGLE SPIES, BUT IN BATTALIONS!"

Interiors of Roger and Orson's libraries. Roger picks up telephone receiver and dials Orson. The telephone rings three times in Orson's dark library with no response, which activates his answering system.

ROGER: Orson, what a wonderful birthday present to hear your voice. You can't know how wonderful until the distant day when you, too, approach ninety.

               The Apostle Paul tells us, via the Corinthians, that three qualities abide: Faith, Hope, and Love. For our prodigal son, the first and the last have never wavered. But hope of a homecoming has dimmed. Time is running out. We must get together soon.

[Lights dim.]

Interior of Roger and Orson's libraries, June 4, 1985. Roger picks up telephone receiver and dials Orson.

ORSON: Hello.

ROGER: Orson, how are you. Is your pinched nerve continuing to cause you pain?

ORSON: Yes, unfortunately. However, it was far worse when I spent those recent months in Paris doing battle in the French courts for my film. I'm still making occasional Kabuki faces at Kiki when the pain becomes particularly severe, looking for a touch of sympathy and receiving none. The truth is that if your mind is with you and you are not in agony, that's being ahead of the game.

ROGER: I've never denied that because, all my life, I've had nothing but luck and the luck continues. It's a year-and-a-half until Halley's Comet and I'm absolutely not going to mumble or moan 'til after that.

ORSON: Here's reason enough for a year and a half of hosannas.

ROGER: Promise not to keep asking me how I am. What we should do in our telephone conversations is for you to talk and me to listen. What you should be doing now is writing your memoir.

ORSON: That's what I'm doing But it's not paying the groceries.

ROGER: No, but it will.

ORSON: I need a few commercials. And I'm doing some other things. I've finished cutting a couple of specials. If I can sell one, it'll be fine. I told you I did a pilot for a series, *Scene of the Crime*. It didn't sell beyond the first six episodes. I foolishly imagined that it was so stupid that it had to sell. [Laughter] It wasn't stupid enough, so that's a blow. Everybody loved the pilot. They had an audience test. They loved it, the sponsor loved it, the client loved it, and the agency loved it, but they found that it was just a little bit different than anything they've ever done, and they were afraid to

put it on. Anything that's slightly different is a
danger because, if it is a failure, everybody is
going to look around for the fellow who suggested
doing it in the first place. I wasn't the fellow in this
instance. I was just hired as an actor. It was a case
of bureaucratic terror over a very minor bit of
originality. The same day I received this news, a
devoted and sweet old gentleman, Ted, older
than you are who takes care of phone calls for me,
irritated an advertising client and I lost a $50,000
job. *When sorrows come, they come not single spies,
but in battalions!* But, I can always turn to you,
you're rich.

ROGER: [Laughs]

ORSON: Thank God I've got a rich old friend.

ROGER: I'm just comfortable.

ORSON: Comfortable for me is rich. And I, an old
           adventurer, can always shuffle along behind you,
           old money bags. Goodbye. I'll call you soon.

[Lights dim.]

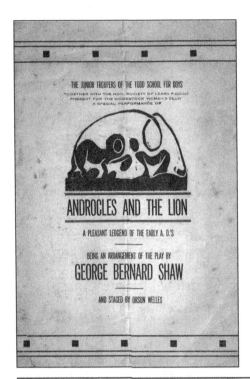

Playbill for the 1930 Todd School production of George Bernard Shaw's *Androcles and the Lion,* staged by and starring Orson.

NOTE

A mystery surrounds the author of this delightful satire. Just what is Bernard Shaw, vegetarian, socialist, anti-vivisectionist and Irishman, really driving at? A number of years ago when "Androcles" first appeared, people stopped hissing him as a propogandist long enough to hail him as a millenial wit. Then the Crown Prince of Austria left in a huff one memorable performance and since then, or rather until the Malvern Festival of 1928, 'G. B. S." and "anarchist" have been synonomous.

Then our Gallic chameleon blushed and gave birth to the metropolitan success "The Apple Cart," his most entertaining contradiction. And then, as the world was persuading itself that there must have been just a big misunderstanding, out came Mr. Shaw again, to announce in the press that he'd been joking all along.

In "Androcles and the Lion" the author flaunts the wormy spots in Ceasarism, Paganism, and Martyrdom right in our faces. But don't let that worry you. Some where in Hertfordshire a blue eye is winking. It is suggested that you wink right back and accept, for this evening at least, the Shavian doctrine of the theatre: "Don't take anything seriously."

PROLOGUE - - AT THE EDGE OF A JUNGLE

ACT I - - - - - A ROAD TO ROME

ACT II BEHIND EMPEROR'S BOX AT COLLISEUM

DRAMATIS PERSONAE

The Emperor	Robert Crane
Metellus	Hasey Tarbox
Mere Patricians	William Dalzell
	Harold Redeker
	Malcom MacDonald
The Captain	Arthur Baldus
The Centurian	Bud Baker
Two Soldiers	Walter Sporlein
	David Light
The Keeper of the Royal Menagerie	Sumner Carruth
The Editor	Robert Scott
Retiavus	Paul Granville
Secutor	Jack Atwood
Other Gladiators	John Lawler
	David Whipple
The Whip	Willis Varner
The Call Boy	Fred Marshall
Assistant Call Boy	Bill Wahl
The Armour Boy	Andrew Weedall
Ropes and Hooks	Dick Norian
	Irving Sunde
Baskets	Edward Karger
Bearers of Imperial Sedan Chair	Sandy Smith
	Francis Graham
An Ox Driver	William Magee
The Christians—	
Lavinia	Harry Struepel
Julia	Betty Hill
Publius	Frank Johnson
Sextus	Charles Barton
Junius	Jack Hodgson
Guliemus	Bill Fine
Marcellus	Walter Borchers
Portius	Richard Turner
Julius	George Dickerson
Marcus	Bob Wahl
Spintho	John Stein
Ferovius	Orson Welles
Androcles	Edgerton Paul
—and his Lion	Frank Mayer

ACT THREE
SCENE FOUR
JUNE 6, 1985
I THINK WE FIRST SPOKE, AND THEN SANG, LATER WE TOLD STORIES, AND FINALLY DANCED

Interior of Roger and Orson's libraries. Roger picks up telephone receiver and dials Orson.

ORSON: Hello.

ROGER: Orson.

ORSON: So, how are you?

ROGER: Fine.

ORSON: How is your updated *Rise and Fall* coming?

ROGER: Sorting through and writing about the past nine decades is an Augean task, and, from time to time, quite encouraging. I've made a good deal of progress during the past month. I was writing this morning about Edwin Embree, about a particularly memorable trip we took with him to New York in the late '40s and stumbled upon the New Year's Eve festivities at Times Square. We were engulfed in that crowd, and saw Guy Lombardo and his band bring in the New Year. Is Lombardo still around?

ORSON: No. He joined the majority about two years ago. But they still manage to play that awful song. Was I with you?

ROGER: Oh, no, just Horty, Edwin, and his wife, Katherine. We saw you a few times at Sardi's and places like that, but I don't think we ever went out on New Year's in New York with you.

ORSON: I never ventured out on New Year's Eve, even in New York, except once, and that time I got in trouble with Virginia. I was preparing a play and we were invited to a New Year's Eve party. I said to her, "I just can't go until I get this finished. You go with Chubby and the others, and enjoy yourself. Call me around New Year's if you feel like it." She left at about ten o'clock. At about eleven-thirty, I heard raucous noise outside and it kind of intrigued me. I thought a moment's rest would be good. So, I went downstairs and took a little walk along Broadway and got near a nightclub which I used to frequent, the Latin Quarter, America's answer to the Moulin Rouge, which prided itself on having the best and the most beautiful dancers in the world. It was owned by the TV woman, Barbara Walters' father, Lou. He had a pretty wife working in the chorus line. I came in and said hello just as everybody was singing, "Should auld acquaintance be forgot, and never brought to mind." We all got in a line and they put two exquisitely gammed dancers on either side of me in their heavy makeup with feathers and no clothes on. I returned home and continued working. The next morning, there I was on the front page of the *Daily News*, sandwiched between these two chorus girls.

ROGER: And you had told Virginia you were working.

ORSON: Yes, I said I had never left. I'd forgotten this brief dalliance. It really didn't seem important that I'd been out for an hour. I told her, "I worked all night, and I'm glad I did." [Laughter] Of course, after she saw the front page, explaining my brief excursion proved challenging. In fact, it led considerably to my subsequent infidelities. [Laughter] That was my only night out on New Year's. You know what they do in Spain on New Year's? They have a famous clock in Madrid, which is the equivalent of the ball in Times Square. It's a time-honored custom, you have twelve white grapes in a glass and, at midnight, at each strike of the clock, you eat a grape until the glass is drained. Everybody all over Spain does that. I hate New Year's myself. Too much drunkenness and not enough thought. It's a damn Scotch invention. Nobody ever really paid any attention to New Year's except the Scottish, and it grew from them. The alcoholic intake on New Year's in Scotland is beyond belief. I was in Edinburgh on a New Year's Eve, so I know what I'm talking about. It looked like the end of the world.

ROGER: I was kind of a two-bit Bobby Burns scholar. I can't remember any New Year's verse of his.

ORSON: I have a terrible hunch that he wasn't very good. But maybe I'm wrong, probably because I can't do the dialect. [Laughter]

ROGER: Are you old enough to remember Harry Lauder?

ORSON: Oh, yes. I remember him.

ROGER: He made a fortune on that dialect.

ORSON: I saw him on megaphone in one of those little shorts that people like George Jessel and Burns and Allen used to do. Terrible voice. But he was a big, great man in vaudeville.

ROGER: That's right. He just had one thing that he milked for years and years.

ORSON: He was one of the highest paid of all the people that was ever booked in vaudeville, and I don't know why people loved him so, but they did.

ROGER: "A bonnie, bonnie lassie."

ORSON: I've never been too keen for Scottish music or folklore. I'm not very fond of any folklore. I think dances are exactly the same all over the world. [Laughing] They just change the costumes. Learn one and you know them all, and join right in. I think they're all based on a couple of basic dances that migrated. One Moorish dance, which became the Morris dance of England, is a particularly shapeless affair. They just hop about like the poorest students of Adolph Bolm. You're lucky you haven't had to sit and watch dancers performing interminably as I was required to do as a special envoy to Mr. Roosevelt, visiting presidents of the Latin American republics. They always took me to the national opera house to see performances of the local ballet troupe, performing dances, which lasted eight and a half hours. I can tell you all about capoeiras, combat dances, of Brazil, and the makuta, a fertility dance, of Trinidad. I've been exposed to a great deal of dance, not just in Latin America, but around the globe, and they're all jiggling almost identically. I have a theory that they're all heavily choreographed by a lady or a gentleman, officials from the government who picked up a few dancing lessons somewhere and adapted the dances for popular entertainment. I have the feeling that dancing is the last thing we did to express ourselves. I think we first spoke, and then sang, later we told stories, and finally we danced.

It just seems logical that the first thing we would do was to grunt and then we would think. But, maybe the first thing we would do was dance before we would grunt. Nobody knows. Thousands of books have been written on the subject. I think children first make an attempt to speak and, then, they make an attempt to chant, because they can't dance. What I find fascinating is what the artists along the Spanish/French border left us. They painted exquisitely sophisticated pictures in dozens of caves. There is no relationship to the primitive art that we know among the Indians, blacks, and Asians. The caves are scattered throughout the Pyrenees, in Southern France and Northern Spain. The Altamira cave in Spain is the finest of them all. Paintings of bison predominate, no doubt homage to the hunt.

ROGER: I read something about a cave that was discovered somewhere in the Basque countryside.

ORSON: That's the Ekain cave. It was discovered in the late '60s. I'd love to see it.

ROGER: You're quite familiar with the Basque country, aren't you?

ORSON: Oh, yes. It's an enchanting place. In the mid-'50s, I produced a series of travel sketches for British television, and one looked at the Basque country.

ROGER: I think I saw some of those programs.

ORSON: I don't think so. I believe they were only aired in England. In the Basque episode, I compared our restless, constantly changing, progress-obsessed, technology-driven culture to the contented, grounded Basques, who have lived for centuries satisfied in a static, agrarian society.

ROGER: Civilization and progress are not always synonymous.

ORSON: Not at all. I made the point in the film that the most civilized nations are those where progress is not a primary obsession. The Basques also have a marvelous attitude toward death, which is captured in one of their proverbs, "Live until you die, and, until then, don't panic." The Basques don't care whether or not a man dies wealthy, but they do care passionately whether or not he dies well, which cues you into your favorite subject.

ROGER: Death, for heaven's sake? It's the subject that you think that I overdo.

ORSON: No, I don't think you overdue it, but it is one that you have faced with a certain gallant loquacity for the past thirty years. [Orson laughs]

ROGER: That's probably true.

ORSON: You have a kind of old Roman stoic view of it.

ROGER: Exactly. It seems to me so silly that we fear it because decrepitude is inevitable. Death seems so desirable once you've had a really fruitful life and there's nothing left but withering and dying— that's the only place, as I see it, where God goofed. Everything else is wonderful. We all are born, we grow, we propagate, we flower, and then we wither and we die. But, it's that penultimate period which is dragged out, and better philosophers than I have talked about it. What I feel is that, not in my lifetime or in yours, there's going to be an entirely different feeling about the whole thing. The wake is so wonderful. After a person has died, friends and family get together and drink to the deceased's life, and sing a few songs. Why can't such a celebration be done ahead of time?

ORSON: You mean invite everybody while you're still with us?

ROGER: Yes. Only a very few would want it. But, those of us who do would call in a mortician—

ORSON: You're going to invite the undertaker to the ceremony?

ROGER: Yes, along with—

ORSON: That's quite a social event. You're going to be there chatting away with the undertaker at your side?

ROGER: Exactly. And, you're going to have a few drinks and a few laughs with your friends, and you're going to say goodbye, and you attend your own wake.

ORSON: A very stoic approach.

ROGER: It isn't stoic. It's because I'm a coward. I hate approaching this decline, which is just inevitable.

ORSON: As Hemingway said, "Every story has an unhappy ending."

ROGER: When you come right down to it, I'm talking suicide, which is unsettling to many people.

ORSON: We always feel resentful to suicides, don't we?

ROGER: Yes. By contrast, the Romans believed there was something noble about suicide. God knows, there is nothing noble about it. But, if a person wants to end his or her life to avoid a painful and prolonged decline, where is the moral turpitude?

ORSON: In other words, you are saying we should be allowed to go at the time of our own choosing?

ROGER: Yes. In recent years, six of our friends have died. With the exception of one, the common refrain of the mourners was, "Wasn't it a blessing?" When you are on top of the mountain, that's the time to go. For those few who want it, you say goodbye, wrap the drapery of your couch about you, and lie down to pleasant dreams.

ORSON: When do you make the decision to end your life, when do you know when the fires are dying?

ROGER: That's the question that's the fault in my whole—

ORSON: Very few people have the strength of character to acknowledge that the fire is really dying. I have a friend who I trust with my life, to whom I've given the power of life and death, and who will visit me in the hospital, and if I'm a vegetable turn something off if that is possible.

ROGER: You can sign a living will, which says that you don't want your life extended by any kind of artificial means.

ORSON: You know, when I say my friend is going to do it, I'm talking about what is not covered by that statement. What I'm talking about is a situation where there isn't a choice, but you're just lying there after a stroke, motionless.

ROGER: What's gained by holding on to our population until everyone is one hundred? Maybe it will be possible, medically, to do that, but is it wise?

ORSON: Wouldn't it be very dangerous, indeed, to start encouraging the dissemination of older people because they are sociologically inconvenient?

ROGER: You're so right. But, I'm talking about a very few who want to make a decision about themselves.

ORSON: Well, we really have two questions here, don't we? One is euthanasia in its various forms, the right not to live when life no longer has significance, ending it with some form of dignity. The other is a cool, pagan, Roman, Japanese kind of suicide.

ROGER: A suicide that is noble in some kind of way, instead of disgraceful. I think you know more about that than I.

ORSON: No, I don't know more about it.

ROGER: Sure you do. You've studied Roman history more than I have.

ORSON: What I think is that the Romans and the Japanese were very concerned with their dignity and their nobility.

ROGER: They were macho.

ORSON: Not exactly macho, but Roman gravitas and honor. That is not a Christian or Jewish moral position, which is why it is rarer in our culture. But, I would imagine that you, without attitudinizing about the Japanese, would be emotionally on their side. There's also the thing you have, luck. Who was it, a revolutionary or a colonial officer who was so lucky and had the famous lines, *Stay thy hand Lord! It is more than enough—more than these can bear!* quoting the *Bible*, of course. In other words, don't give me any more good luck. And, I suspect that's how you feel. You've had so much that you almost can't bear the thought of more.

ROGER: Let's face it; it's a type of fear.

ORSON: What do you mean?

ROGER: Well, the luck can't last. In *Time and Chance*, I wrote that my entire life has been a matter of luck, and it starts out with a verse from Ecclesiastes.

ORSON: How does it go?

ROGER: "For I looked again and saw under the sun that the race is not to the swift. Nor the battle to the strong, nor yet riches to the men of understanding, but time and chance happeneth to all." And it happeneth very happily to me. It's a weakness probably, not to want to get the dirty end of the stick at the end of life.

ORSON: What do you think death is?

ROGER: Sleep, a very wished for and blessed sleep and nothing more. We're not going to have any reincarnation. We had our chance. Good Lord, one season on earth, isn't that enough? Isn't it silly to think that we're going to come back?

ORSON: You would feel sorry to be surprised?

ROGER: (Laughs) I think so, yes.

ORSON: Just imagine any form of immortality. You would be sorry to find that that existed?

ROGER: I can't imagine anything but sorrow in looking back on the hopes you had that didn't materialize. I'd like to end with hope. You, in no small measure, are responsible for my decades-long ruminations on death, beginning when we used to read of the deaths in the *Bible*, which are some of the most poignant in literature. For instance, the death of David, who had been such a sexual giant. They put the beautiful Shunammite maiden, Abishag, in his bed. Remember the passage, "Now King David was old and stricken in years; and they covered him with clothes, but he gat no heat." Shakespeare on death is also worth attending. Falstaff, which you've played so beautifully since your youth, can bring tears to my eyes. In *Henry V* when Nell Quickly reaches up and says—

ORSON: "So a' bade me lay more clothes on his feet: I put my hand into the bed and felt them, and they were as cold as any stone;"

ROGER: "Then I felt his knees, and they were as cold as any stone,"

ORSON: "And so upward and upward, and all was as cold as any stone."

ROGER: "As cold as any stone." It's so poignant. It's scared me all my life.

ORSON: Well, I won't keep you any longer, but it was lovely talking to you.

ROGER: As always, it was great.

ORSON: Bye.

[Lights dim.]

ACT THREE
SCENE FIVE
AUGUST 19, 1985
I WISH I WERE MORE BUSY MAKING PICTURES

Interior of Roger and Orson's libraries. Orson picks up telephone receiver and dials Roger.

ORSON: Roger?

ROGER: Good, good, good!

ORSON: Is that a recording saying good, good, good?

ROGER: No. I came in when I heard your voice. Where have you been, in Canada?

ORSON: No. I'm in the Sun Belt. I didn't get to go to Canada. I lost my voice. My vocal cords are swollen, but nothing else, luckily. No one really knows how to treat the problem except in New York where they have an opera company. Don't worry. It's time you came out here for a visit.

ROGER: Soon.

ORSON: You keep stalling and saying soon you'll come visit me, and your soons are extending into infinity.

ROGER: We are both so busy—

ORSON: I wish I were more busy making pictures rather than spending inordinate amounts of time at film festivals, in hotels, and in restaurants performing a dancing bear act beseeching potential backers for money. Bring your *Rise and Fall* work in progress and work on it here. Come cheer up a lonely vagabond who misses you.

ROGER: I'll come out, but not before the fall. I'll check my calendar and you do the same.

ORSON: I will my dear and illusive friend. If I can't get you to come sooner, I must be content to wait.

ROGER: I'll do my damnedest to stay in one piece until then. Being in one piece at my age makes me a curiosity to many, and far more than a curiosity to widows. For some inexplicable reason, I prove to be a magnet to women far my junior.

ORSON: Isn't that wonderful!

ROGER: The boldness of widows. It's unbelievable.

ORSON: [Roars.]

ROGER: Yesterday, at breakfast, a fairly young-looking gal, immaculately and expensively dressed said to me, "Excuse me; I've been looking at you. You're the most unusual man I have ever seen. I just had to introduce myself." I couldn't think of a clever instant retort. But, what I'm going to say in the future is something like, "Okay, kid, I'm available. What's your net worth?" Some of them are rich and they're looking for amorous adventure. Why the hell don't I cash in on it?

ORSON: Yes, my God! All you'd have to do is take a short tour to Florida and you could be leaving your descendants billions. They have no shame at all,

and, if you notice, it's the women, not the
men, who lose their inhibitions after a certain
age.

ROGER: It certainly seems to be.

ORSON: They turn into creatures that would have shocked
themselves to their bones when they were young
and beautiful. So, how have you been?

ROGER: Pretty good.

ORSON: Did I tell you that I was invited recently to have a
private audience with Pope John Paul II and I
couldn't accept it?

ROGER: Really?

ORSON: Yes. I must say I admire the Pope. I think his visit
with his assassin was very touching. Did you see it
on television? He went to the prison in Rome
where all the terrorists are kept and he spent an
hour with the man who tried to kill him. They just
held on to each other and talked as though they
were loving brothers. Then, he took a long time
talking intimately with all those people who have
killed women and children with bombs. I read
three of his poems on the air for the Vatican not
long ago, and they are beautiful.

ROGER: In what language?

ORSON: I read them in Italian. They had been written in
Polish, and they were awfully good in Italian.
Moving. You knew that he was an actor?

ROGER: No.

ORSON: Yes, in his youth, he was surrounded by actors. Our Pope was a professional actor and something of a bohemian before he took his Holy Orders.

ROGER: How did he learn all these languages?

ORSON: He's famous for knowing so many languages because nobody will ever learn Polish. [Laughter] It's the ugliest language in the world, whereas Russian is the most beautiful, and in self-defense, the Poles all learn it. The Poles know two languages besides their own by the time they're ten. Once you've learned another language well, the third is easier, the fourth is easier still. The Pope speaks good German and English, and, of course, he's surrounded by a lot of angry Italians. [Laughter] While he was enrolled at Poland's Jagiellonian University in the late '30s, he participated in an experimental troupe called Studio 38. He was torn between choosing a life in theatre arts or in the Church. The Nazi occupation closed the university and the future Pope labored in a quarry and, later, in a chemical factory to support himself and dodge deportation to Germany. When the university reopened after the war, he reconnected with Studio 38. However, his father took a dim view of the theatre and encouraged his son to become a priest. After the old man's death, his son, as an act of homage to his father, entered the priesthood. I have talked to old Polish actors who say he could have been a great actor, and his poetry is superb. I read it pretty well and he heard it and said he'd like to see me.

ROGER: I think that it's an important thing for you to do. I think you should.

ORSON: But two Popes have already received me. I admire the current Pope. But, I don't have the time now. If he wants to see me when I'm in Rome, I'd be delighted. The first Pope I got to see was Pacelli, Pius XII, shortly after the war. He had a kind of El Greco face and was very aristocratic. He had dry hands like a lizard and he held my hand in his two hands for forty minutes while we talked, and all his questions revolved around Hollywood gossip: "Is Irene Dunne really going to have a divorce?" "Who is Van Heflin seeing?" All he wanted was the gossip. [Great laughter.]

ROGER: Well, he couldn't get it in his confession booth.

ORSON: He wanted it from the horse's mouth. After our decidedly temporal visit, I was then taken around the Vatican by the Acting Secretary of State, who became the next Pope. He took me everywhere in the Vatican because I was the first real star that visited after the war. I was a big novelty and the Vatican had an elaborate itinerary laid out. We went upstairs and downstairs and in my ladies chamber and we saw every artwork. It was a very hot day and I knew he would have loved to stop and I would have loved to stop, but he couldn't think of any way to do it. We passed a statue and he said that Eamon De Valera, who was then the Prime Minister of Ireland—remember him?

ROGER: I remember him, of course.

ORSON: He said that De Valera, a week earlier, had been to the Vatican and admired the statue. I was so tired that I carelessly asked a profoundly stupid question of the second ranking member of the Vatican and acting Secretary of State, *"Eamon è Cattolico?"* The

Acting Secretary of State looked back at me and said, "*Un Cattolico fanatico!*" [Laughter] Isn't that a wonderful answer? "*Fanatico!*" The Italians take their Catholicism so very much less seriously than the Irish do.

ROGER: I thought that the Irish took their religion with a grain of salt.

ORSON: Oh, no. They're the most devout. They think a priest is somebody superior to other people. If there's a meeting of the town about the sewer system, school system, or any damn thing, the priests are there and considered as the great authorities on any subject that is public. That isn't true in any other Catholic country. An irascible character that worked for us in Italy would stand in our garden with a hose watering the flowers and when a priest happened to come along the path, he would spray him with water and then say, "Oh, I'm so sorry, father, I didn't see you." [Laughter.] That could never happen in Ireland.

ROGER: The Americans seem to have mostly Irish priests.

ORSON: Yes. That's why the Irish have become much more liberal. The Catholic Church in America was wonderful about the atomic bomb, I thought, when they officially condemned nuclear weapons on moral grounds.

ROGER: What do you mean?

ORSON: I thought you read papers. You do nothing except go over your old papers laboring on *The Rise and Fall?* [Laughter] You must have read about it, how all the bishops in America got together and, with only a few holdouts, wrote a pastoral letter, *The*

Challenge of Peace, condemning nuclear weapons. No other religion has taken that stand. Am I boring you?

ROGER: Not at all.

ORSON: Before I risk doing so, I'll bid you a good evening.

ROGER: Good night.

[Lights dim.]

ACT THREE
SCENE SIX

SEPTEMBER 8, 1985
I'M NOT IMMUNE TO THE HORRORS OF OLD AGE

Interior of Roger and Orson's libraries. Orson picks up telephone receiver and dials Roger.

ROGER: Hello.

ORSON: Roger?

ROGER: Old man Hill here.

ORSON: I want to object to the obscene literature that I've been getting. [Laughter] God, the "Big Ox" brochure you sent and your marginalia certainly livened my day. I didn't know it was from you initially because I threw the envelope away. So here I am seriously scanning this "Big Ox" potency enhancer brochure, and I'm wondering who the hell would send me this and why would he write sardonic asides in red ink and take such an interest in my libido? Then I recognized your florid script. [Uproarious laughter] It's quite funny.

ROGER: You finally received something in the mail that might be of interest.

ORSON: It's worthy of your best efforts when you were in the advertising business, particularly the end that reads, "Of course Big Ox won't give you an erection. You'll need a woman for that." [More laughter]

ROGER: But, what I can't understand is how they chose the name, "Big Ox" for God's sakes, an ox is a castrated bull.

ORSON: But Big Ox sounds so virile. There are no depths too low to which advertising people will sink to make a buck in America. I received another piece of junk mail, which promised that if I were to ingest their nostrum on a regular basis, I would feel blissful and live forever. All these things are simply combinations of—

ROGER: Vitamins.

ORSON: Quackery has been thriving since the beginning of recorded time and is likely to flourish as long as man remains easy to fleece.

ROGER: [Laughter] Did you ever go to Lourdes?

ORSON: No. But I've been told by people who've gone, who were not dizzy with faith, that the greatest miracle in Lourdes is that everybody doesn't come down with some terrible disease from getting into the uncirculated water with their fellow faithful.

ROGER: Look what Mary Baker Eddy did with the concept of mind over matter. Her brand of magic has seduced millions. God knows there's something to Christian Science. "As a man thinketh, so is he" has a great deal of truth to it. You can talk yourself into trouble.

ORSON: Have you read that fellow Cousins' book? He used to be the editor of *The Saturday Review*.

ROGER: No.

ORSON: He's written two books. I've read his newest one. He had a terminal illness with about three months to go, and he cured himself by reading all the funniest books he could find, and watching comedies. He thought positively, and laughed himself right out of the hospital.

ROGER: No kidding?

ORSON: Then, he had another terminal illness about two years ago, and he did the same thing. The doctors are convinced that he's right. I know Norman Cousins. He's a very nice guy, not at all a nut.

ROGER: Speaking of positive thinking, do you remain optimistic about finding funding for a project or two: *Cradle, Big Brass Ring, The Dreamers? Lear, The Other Side of the Wind,* or *The Magic Show?*

ORSON: The French government assures me it is very close to funding *Lear.* My troubles with the Iranian backer for *The Other Side of the Wind* could be coming to an end, which would allow me to finish editing the film that is agonizingly close to being complete. *Cradle* is not dead. New potential backers want to meet with me. Only a few more segments of *The Magic Show* need to be filmed and, after a bit more postproduction, it will be finished. I've had to say no to any number of acting jobs to work on these projects. However, I did accept an uncomplicated audio job for the Japanese. Did I tell you about their offer?

ROGER: No.

ORSON: Oh, this is so crazy and so interesting. The Japanese are offering me a hundred thousand dollars for ninety minutes of my life on tape, not video, just audio. Gary Graver just came in now to talk about it.

ROGER: Great. That's what I've been so anxious for you to do.

ORSON: It's good to hear your voice. I didn't hear from you for a couple of days and I began to worry.

ROGER: Don't worry on my account.

ORSON: I rejoice on your account and only worry when I don't hear your voice. Before this call comes to a close, did your doctor find any heart problems?

ROGER: No.

ORSON: It's just high blood pressure?

ROGER: That's all. What about your health? You are always so elliptical on the subject when I ask.

ORSON: I'm not immune to the horrors of old age. As you know, my doctor grabbed my attention a while ago when he told me my heart wasn't functioning properly, my liver was a mess, and that my blood pressure was off the chart. He said, "Either you lose weight or you will die." No equivocation. So, for months I've been dieting. If you'll pardon the pun, I've gone cold turkey, eating little and what little I eat is dispiritingly unappetizing.

ROGER: I had no idea about your doctor's dire comments. Why didn't you tell me earlier?

ORSON: I didn't want you to worry. It's a boring subject. Not only have I given up all the food I love, I've had to abandon coffee, and substitute Perrier for vodka.

ROGER: Are you seeing results and feeling better?

ORSON: I've lost over fifty pounds and feel worse.

ROGER: How so?

ORSON: I've lost a good deal of energy, and I hope to God
           it comes back because there's so much that needs
           my attention. In addition to the intrinsic joy of
           eating well, dining provides an ideal opportunity
           for spirited social discourse. Even when I'm dining
           with others, I feel alone and removed. This is one
           of the many reasons why I look forward to your
           next visit. You eat next to nothing and I won't be
           tempted to covet what you consume. Call me, okay?

ROGER: Yes.

ORSON: Bye.

   [Lights dim.]

*September 22, 1985, Roger dials Orson's telephone number. It rings
three times, Orson is absent, which activates Orson's recorded message.*

ORSON: [Recorded message] Please leave a message. Orson.

ROGER: [Roger leaves the following voice mail message to
           Orson] Orson, sorry I missed you and, as a result,
           I'm constrained to leave this message. You may
           remember that my father was constantly being
           "constrained" to speak out about something on his
           mind. In this morning's mail was the letter from
           your classmate, Guggie, asking about you. We hear
           from Paul about every five years and always under
           some new medical corporate letterhead. I told you
           I think of the time, some years ago, we sent out as

Christmas greetings, the early page of *Time and Chance*. The text begins, "This is the posthumous greeting to my grandchildren." Assuming I had died, Guggie replied with a treasured letter of condolence to Hortense and overblown praise of me, his lifetime idol. I had the Tom Sawyer fun of peeking in at my own funeral. If I don't hear from you later today, I'll call you tomorrow.

[Lights dim.]

ACT THREE
SCENE SEVEN
SEPTEMBER 30, 1985
NOW I DREAM OF SOMETHING THAT MAY PROVE HARDER TO ATTAIN—GREAT HAPPINESS

Interior of Orson and Roger's libraries. Roger's telephone rings.

ROGER: [Voice Message: This is Roger Hill. Leave a message after the beep.]

ORSON: Roger, are you on the lam? This would seem to indicate a stay with us here in Los Angeles or Las Vegas is in order, for hiding out purposes if nothing else. Nobody will find you in either location. They can never find me! But for God's sake, let us hear from you.

[Lights dim.]

Interior of Roger and Orson's libraries, later that day. Roger leaves Orson a phone message.

ROGER: Orson, sorry I missed your call. I've spent a lifetime on the lam. Let's set a date for my next trip west. Either Los Angeles or Las Vegas would be fine. By now, you should have received the small packet of your youthful letters. But, since I mailed that sampling of your letters, I've had time to uncover stuff long misplaced or forgotten, as well as time to organize, annotate, and index, and have those items ready for you in a portable file, which I'll bring out with me. Then you'll have much, if not most, of your childhood literary efforts returned to you.

I wondered if a dimly remembered Sherlock Holmes radio play you wrote in Shanghai and mailed to Woodstock was still extant. Ah, so. More important, I turned up a copy of *Marching Song*. For my money, it remains a compelling, if overly long, play. If that God-awful *Hearts of Age*—memories of your stumbling repeatedly on that absent step on the Wallingford fire escape, and your bloody shin—is worth saving, *Marching Song*, written two years earlier, should rate a Pulitzer. At least it's worth publication.

World Premiere of *Marching Song*, June 7, 1950.

A set from Marching Song.

Take care of your early correspondence. As Hascy said, when I was entertaining a group by reading one of your illustrated letters from Africa, "This stuff is fascinating. It's also incredible for a teenager. It must end up in some great library where it can never be lost." Talk to you soon.

[Center downstage behind a translucent scrim seventeen-year-old Orson is sitting up on a bed reading a letter he has just composed.]

Dear Skipper:

One look at Africa was enough—or rather, not enough. Yes, I've deserted the ship, I've cut myself off from everything including communication and the English language, and for the month, I'm here on the Dark Continent, whether I like it or not. I like it. It's very new, everything here, and quite as exciting as an adventure story from the Arabian Nights. Exciting is the word. There is nothing sullen or mysterious or Oriental about Marrakesh. The oldest city in Morocco and the thickest populated, the greatest African Oasis and the last. (Camel caravans trudge in under the high, pink archways, night and day from Soudan and the Senegal and

Timbuktu.) The pleasure city of the Bedouin, the mountain clansmen and the Grand Caid, the high capital of Islamic fanaticism; frenzied, noisy, wicked, utterly proud, a violent place. I have been lying here in bed brooding over the typewriter which I have perched on my knees in the frantically peach-colored French quilts, trying to frame sentences for you about this wild, swaggering city. OASIS is one word. This is the Arab's Broadway. STRONGHOLD is another. This is the last great stronghold of barbarism. There is aristocracy here, but not civilization. There is neither the mechanical boredom of the western metropolis nor the splendid languor of the Far East. There are princes here and craftsmen and slaves (and these are the elements of culture) but, somehow they have never managed sophistication. Eight hundred years ago Yakub al-Mansur raised the great Koutoubia. It is a mighty and awesome minaret; some call it the loveliest of the world's towers. Yet it is a ruin without venerability. One sees it age and crumble with regret, but without tears. I think that is because there are no tears in Marrakesh. There is no antiquity—and Marrakesh is older than the written word of history, older than time—but time is that which it has yet to achieve.

This is the first I have written down about Africa and it's coming out slowly on the paper with apparent effort. Every sentence is punctuated by an arid half an hour. Between this and the last, even a good five minutes. I sit here wondering how long O, Lord until some sleep-hungry neighbor starts up a peevish rat-tatting on my chamber wall. The shutters of my windows are thrown open. It's a garden-scented, star-populous, moon-bright and very noisy night. A million dogs from the Mellah to the Medinah howl without pause; locusts, gramophones, flutes, drums, cymbals, crowing cocks, the sleighbellish ringing of the taxi carriages, hoarse Arabic and nasal French, music and more music. This is the eve of the Aid-Kibur, the big feast of the Moslem world; a night to be out in the streets. But tomorrow I must be up at dawn and see the Sultan pass in state on his way to prayer.

Well, the lady on the other side of the wall behind me has put her shoes out in the hall and closed the door with emphasis. She is banging about now and coughing in no uncertain a tone. I leave the typewriter silent and the coughing stops. Every punch it takes to tell you this is an insult to French respectability. Cats have begun to cry under our windows. The little hotel has rolled itself up in an offensive silence. Outside, beyond the orange grove, in the city, the tumult persists.

It's been two whole days now since I allowed that wretched woman in the next room to shut me up on what promised to be some of the completest drivel I have ever spouted. It's early evening, just before dinner. There's a superb sunset out on the desert and I should be cabbing madly to the oasis to visit it. But one has to draw the line somewhere. I've been visiting sunsets and Kasbahs and Souks and whatnot, just about enough. In a mere week, I've spent most of my money and all of my time doing just what I swore to you I wouldn't. Don't blame me, blame Africa.

Tomorrow I'm getting on a bus and going to Fez, via Rabat and Meknès. I shall settle somewhere and grow horribly industrious and economical.

Love,
Orson

[Lights dim.]

Interior of Roger and Orson's libraries, October 8, 1985. Orson leaves Roger a phone message.

ORSON: Thank you for the package of memorabilia. Much of it I'll weave into my narrative. You know my feelings about mirror gazing, but when reflecting on the past, your own past, it's inevitable. It's taken me a lifetime to begin confronting and considering my past, particularly my mistakes. If I've learned anything over the past seventy years, it's that as you tramp through life, you leave a littered trail of misjudgments. An early misstep was certainly the unraveling of my relationship with Virginia, caused in no small measure by the seduction of the Big World's allure and the intoxication of adulation. From the personal kaleidoscope you sent, I'm holding a copy of a letter you wrote when Virginia and I were separated, telling me a truth that's taken a lifetime to finally appreciate.

[Scrim: Orson reads letter]

Dear Orson,

Hortense has a heart-rending letter of ineffable sweetness and real maturity from Virginia. She says she needs Hortense, so, of course, a bag is being packed.

But it's you, dear beloved that our hearts yearn for. You say you have thought this thing out. Still, I urge you now to give Time, that great mellower, a chance and don't rush now into a final decree.

Your real need, I feel, is not for fewer ties; it is for greater ones. Maybe you will find these elsewhere. I only know you must find them someplace. A real home with its attendant sacrifices is a necessity in your life. Just as it is in mine. Take this from an old wanderer turned Benedict.

I have a clear hunch, nay a deep conviction, that Welles, as a solo wonder-worker will never be truly happy. You are building the structure of your life to great heights. For that very reason, it needs great breadth of base if it isn't to topple.

Forgive me, I'm preaching. It's a habit I've foresworn, at least with you. But my dream for our foster son used to be of great success. Now I dream of something that may prove harder to attain: great happiness.

We love you very, very much,

R

[Lights dim.]

ORSON: Roger, thank you for that long ago sermon of love and for a lifetime of wisdom and happiness that you've given this restless, but ever obedient servant. I'll call you soon.

[Lights dim.]

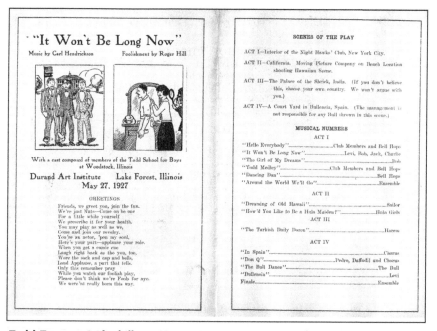

Todd Troupers' playbill, "It Won't Be Long Now," performed at the Durand Art Institute, Lake Forest, Illinois, May 27, 1927

CAST OF CHARACTERS

Bob Warfield, in search of his dream girl...................Donald Topliff
Jim Bailey, his pal with troubles of his own..................Orson Welles
Sam Levi, pants maker by trade (but he traded trades)......................
....Jerome Niederman
Tobias Thompson, who has all the money and a good deal of the
    fun...Jack Marshall
Peggy, his daughter, in love with Jim, but don't tell Toby...................
....Herbert Knowles
Daffodil Dotty, she wants the men to call her "Little Daffy" and
    they all agree she is..Harry Carruth
    The above six characters are carried throughout the plot.

SPECIAL CHARACTERS FOR THE DIFFERENT ACTS

ACT I

Charlie Grant, Daffodil's first victim.............................Charles Rioch
Other Club Members....Harris LeRoy, Paul Olsen, Nelson Leonard,
    Carl Petersmyer, John Hanley.

BELL HOP CHORUS

or as the old Musical Comedy Programs had it, Gentlemen of
    the Ensemble.
Arthur Rice, John Dexter, Ralph Modjeska, Jim Wiggins, Bill
    Wiggins, Robert Hicks, Sherman Perlman, Arthur Smith
The Little Specialty Dancer....................................Homer Spears

ACT II

Mack Sennet, in search of "Miss Lake Forest" or something...........
....John Hanley
The Sailor, He's not really a sailor but he borrowed a sailor hat........
....Charles Rioch
Hula Maidens, in person. Watch for this............Oh what difference
    does it make what their names are. Besides their families may
    find out about it.

ACT III

El Goofus...Charles Rioch
Harem...................Messrs. Barsumian, McCornack, Mayer, MacIntyre

ACT IV

Don Pedro, walking delegate of the Bull Fighters' Union..Chas Rioch.
His Pal, if such a dirty bum can be said to have a pal....John Hanley
His Daughter, but you'd never know it..........................Harris LeRoy
The Dream Girl, Ah, the shero, have your flowers ready....Paul Olsen
The Bull, front legs and points North............................Arthur Smith
The Same Bull, rear legs and contiguous portions....Sherman Perlman
Spanish Chorus....Same as Bell Hop Chorus (or maybe a little worse)

ACT THREE
SCENE EIGHT
OCTOBER 9, 1985
DISAPPOINTMENTS CONTINUE TO AFFECT MY
CONFIDENCE—BUT NEVER MY RESOLVE

Interior of Roger and Orson's libraries, 9:00 p.m. Orson picks up telephone receiver and dials Roger.

ROGER: Hello.

ORSON: Hello, Roger. Did you receive the message of gratitude and love I left on your machine yesterday?

ROGER: Yes. I called you an hour ago and there was no response. I was going to call you later this evening.

ORSON: I've just returned from dinner at the company cafeteria, Ma Maison. It's been a long day and I'm beat. I just wanted to call hoping to convince you to set a date for your long-delayed visit. I need your energy, as it always has, to spark my own.

ROGER: You sound weary.

ORSON: I am, but will admit it to no one but you. My God, Roger, I look as drained as I feel.

ROGER: What do you mean? You've taken, at long last, to looking into the mirror?

ORSON: No, I still continue to avoid mirrors as much as possible. The cause of my lament is *People* magazine.

One of their photographers spent some time with me a few weeks ago for a story they're planning. I received proofs the other day, and I was shaken to my bones. I look like Karl Gerhardt's death mask of Ulysses S. Grant.

ROGER: You're sounding positively stygian.

ORSON: Well, your voice has ushered in the light. I'm glad I caught you, my ever-elusive friend. Last night I finished reading our Paleocene correspondence. One letter, I want to include in my book, a letter I wrote from New York after you and Hortense left and I continued to peddle our *Marching Song* to producers.

ROGER: If it's nearby, read it to me.

ORSON: I won't read the whole thing, but what caught my attention is that it points out the child is father to the man is this passage:

[Scrim: eighteen-year-old Orson reads letter.]

"I am aware that disappointments, it matters not how many, should in no way affect my confidence, but they do. Today, for example, it was neither a shock nor a sense of failure, just the realization of a fact, the cementing of a profound conviction. I refer to Ben Boyar's returning the manuscript. I wasn't even surprised. He said, 'It's a swell show. It makes good reading. It would make a good book. I think maybe it's even a good play. But that doesn't matter. It won't make money. It isn't a commercial piece. At least that's what I think. Maybe I'm wrong.' He thanked me for letting him read it, nicely, I thought, repeating himself, and said goodbye."

Five decades later, disappointments continue to affect my confidence—but never my resolve.

Another letter I sent you not long afterward, on
the American Export Lines' freighter, the *S.S.
Exermont* heading for Morocco, describes my
mood, in verse, and served as a metaphor for how
I viewed the crossing and the world at seventeen.

ROGER: Is it within arm's reach?

ORSON: Yes, it's somewhere on my desk.

[Scrim: Seventeen-year-old Orson reads poem.]

Days now numberless it seems to me
We've lolled and wallowed in a lusty sea.
Time is a thing that used to be.

The order and ascent of days is nothing now;
A March-blown ocean mauls our ploughing prow,
Acreage hysterical for us to plow.

Crash in the galley. Crashes are constant now;
Shiver the empty *Exermont* from screw to prow.
Time is a thing that used to be;
The order and ascent of days is nothing now.

ROGER: Days are numberless and their ascent means little
           in our youth, how true.

ORSON: In old age, they are preciously numbered and their
           descent mocks our dreams and our mortality.

ROGER: Old age is a time of remembering, rejoicing in
           what was, and occasionally regretting what wasn't.

ORSON: Speaking of the former, here are a few lines from a
           prehistoric missive of mine to you when I landed
           in New York to read the part of Marchbanks in

Shaw's *Candida* for Katharine Cornell, all thanks
to your introducing me to Thornton Wilder at
one of Hazel Buchbinder's salons in Chicago.

ROGER: How well I remember the next day, your impromptu
and impassioned dash from Woodstock to New
York. When Thornton realized that you were the
young man who made such an impression on the
Irish stage at sixteen that was reported throughout
Europe and America, he let you know that Cornell
was searching for you to audition for her company.
Yes, that chance encounter with Thornton was the
springboard to your first notable part on the
American stage.

*[Scrim: Eighteen-year-old Orson in a hotel room sitting at a table
takes a page from a typewriter and reads.]*

Dear Skipper,

This is to invoke on you a special blessing from the Gods. You have
never been kinder, sweeter, or more obliging and I have never
passed so serene a Pullman night... The train was nice with good
food in an Edwardian diner, and lots of wonderful people going to
Washington including Ruth Hanna McCormick, and Sect.
Perkins, and Kellogg. I am a New Yorker now by about two hour's
residence, frigid-aired and thoroughly air-conditioned highly
hopeful for absolutely anything—or absolutely nothing....

What I'm getting at is my gratitude, which is boundless. My God,
Skipper, I owe you my life! It was sad leaving you, but you'll be
coming out soon, and pretty soon we'll be going off together,
losing some of that equilibrium of yours...

I have been lollying here, comfortably showered and shaven and
unpacked, phoning. Alex Woollcott is the only one I talked to
personally—he was colossally nice, and we are breakfasting early

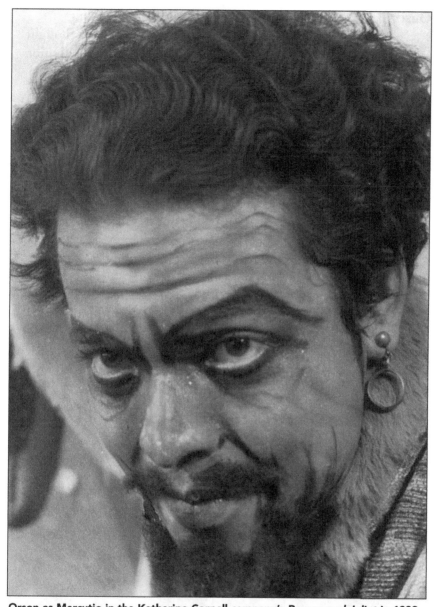

Orson as Mercutio in the Katharine Cornell company's *Romeo and Juliet* in 1933.

next week—but the rest of them are only a matter of time, and not so much of it, they will call me, they will be delighted, even their secretaries are nice. It will all be very thrilling and I might even get a break. Anyway, I go to dinner with a nice shirt on and a high, high heart. Orson

ORSON: How young I once was. Today I am feeling disastrously old. The mind boggles at the thought that you have always been twenty years my senior. But then, in the best sense, you will always be younger than I was when I first checked into Clover Hall. But neither of us can deny that we both suffer the curse of excessive years. De Gaulle likened old age to a shipwreck. Isn't that wonderful? He's so right. We can, in our declining years, either sink slowly, clutching to hope and fighting like hell to hold on, or we can sink swiftly in panic and despair. Like a tenacious bulldog, I continue to fight the good fight to find the money to complete a few of my films and begin *Lear* and *Cradle*.

Orson, in the spring of 1926, third from the left in the middle row, with a clutch of his classmates on the Todd campus in front of Rogers Hall.

The Todd Seminary for Boys faculty in front of Rogers Hall, 1931. Noble Hill is far left, Coach Toney Roskie is to his left, Hortense Hill is fourth from the left, and Roger Hill is fourth from the right.

Clover Hall, 1926   Entrance to Wallingford Hall

ROGER: I would like to live long enough to see *The Other Side of the Wind* and *The Magic Show* completed. I fear I'm too old to ever see your *Lear* and *Cradle*. But, I'll have no regrets if I don't live to see any more of your pictures because I've experienced so very much of your work—your playing Christ at eleven, directing *Julius Caesar* at thirteen, your New York stage productions in your late teens and early twenties: *Voodoo Macbeth, Doctor Faustus,* and *Cradle*, most of your radio programs, and all the films you directed. My only regret is that I never saw your *Around the World in Eighty Days*, either in Boston or New York. Horty and I planned to be with you on opening night in both cities, but the press of school matters kept us in Woodstock. From all accounts, of all your work on the stage, none was more spectacular in size, or more star-crossed than that production.

ORSON: Or costly. We almost had to cancel opening night in Boston.

ROGER: Oh, the costume fiasco.

ORSON: Yes. Cole Porter wrote the score and convinced me that Mike Todd had the money and moxie to produce it. Mike agreed to back the production, but unbeknownst to me, he was broke and backed out.

ROGER: I thought that when the show was well into rehearsal, he learned that your staging pyrotechnics included a flowing oil well, and he pulled out in panic at what he imagined the final production would cost.

ORSON: No, Mike just didn't have the money. He wasn't our only backer, Alexander Korda invested $125,000. I've forgotten how much I invested, but, no matter, our expenses exceeded our resources. I once even had to borrow money from Shorty to pay the actors. *Around the World* was anything but minimalist. Nine carloads of scenery. Movies, slides, a train wreck in miniature, an eagle that flew off with the leading man, a complete Japanese Circus, and a slide from the balcony to the stage. But, no oil well. When we opened in New York, a reviewer joked that the only thing missing in the production was a kitchen sink, so I lugged one on stage the following night.

ROGER: What an extravaganza. I have the records to your show somewhere.

ORSON: You're one of the few. When Todd learned that Porter was writing the music for the show, he winced and said "Cole's finished, there's nothing left in him." "That can't be true of Cole, he's too talented," I said, and I was right, except his next smash hits were in *Kiss Me Kate* that ran the following year. [Laughter] Unfortunately for us, Cole didn't write even one song for *Around the World* that people could remember and hum after leaving the theatre.

ROGER: I remember your telling me that when Todd backed out, you had to finance much of the production.

ORSON: Yes. Many of my projects have foundered for the lack of financial resources. In the mid '50s, I began financing and shooting *Don Quixote*. Coupled with having to scurry for financing, it wasn't long before a gaggle of howling critics began demanding to know when it would be finished. Novelists and biographers aren't asked every other day, "When are you going to finish your book?" As you know better than anyone, Quixote and Sancho Panza took a grip on my imagination in my youth. Over the years, I kept changing the movie and throwing pieces away. You remember, I came close to completing the film, with Quixote journeying to the moon, at about the time astronauts actually accomplished the feat. That spoiled the movie and I threw away ten reels.

ROGER: What's the focus now?

ORSON: The film now centers on the pollution and corruption of old Spain and hope for a new Spain. It's developed into a very personal essay, which I'm renaming, *When Are You Going to Finish Don Quixote?*

ROGER: What a wonderfully comic and bittersweet designation.

ORSON: I should do a similar renaming of *The Other Side of the Wind.*

ROGER: "It's all a matter of money" should be the subject of another of your personal essays.

ORSON: I could write the definitive book on the subject. On the subject of personal essays, I'm considering a chapter in my book on acting.

ROGER: Your acting, or acting in general?

ORSON: Both. I was writing yesterday on the difference between performing before a live audience and before a camera.

ROGER: Is there a great deal of difference between the two?

ORSON: A considerable difference. I am frequently asked
that question and offer up two actors who give the
lie to everything we ever hear about the differences,
which is that the closer you are to the camera lens,
the smaller your effects must be, and that when
acting on a stage your effects must be broader.
That's considered the gospel, but it simply isn't so,
except perhaps in the minds of second-, third-, or
fourth-rate actors. Two of the greatest actors I've
known, and whom I'll use as exemplars to prove
my thesis are Jimmy Cagney and Eduardo De
Filippo.

ROGER: Everyone will know Cagney. But, who will know
De Filippo? I don't.

ORSON: You should. Didn't I take you and Hortense to one
of his plays when you visited me in Italy?

ROGER: No.

ORSON: I'm sorry I cheated you of a rare experience.
Eduardo was more than a great Neapolitan actor;
he was an author and director. He had a long tragic
Picasso-Blue Period face. On the stage, he was vir-
tually immobile, but projected epic authority. The
word spellbinding is so overused that it has become
suspect, but no better word describes how he held
his audience in the old Italian theatres that seated
up to three thousand people. His filling the seats
was particularly remarkable given that Italians are
not constituted to sit in theatres. They prefer to
live out their own private theatre. [Laughter] They
have contempt for the actors on stage being paid to
do something they know they can do with greater
flair. As a result, Italian audiences never shut up, or
applaud, except for Eduardo. Though he's a theatre
actor, he has appeared in many films, without

Eduardo De Filippo

much distinction. He doesn't come alive on film. Cagney is De Filippo's complete opposite. He is a commanding film presence. No actor was ever more animated and convincing.

ROGER: You'll mention a few of your Mercury actors, won't you?

ORSON: Oh, more than a few, as well as a number of actors I've been fortunate to work with over the years. Did I tell you that Joe Cotten has written his autobiography and asked me to look at it before he sends it to his publisher?

ROGER: How does it read?

ORSON: Gentle, witty, and, self-effacing, just like Joe. My only complaint is that it's too brief. He's too sparing of his early successes on the stage. In addition to his wonderful work at the Mercury, he appeared, in 1938, opposite Katharine Hepburn in *The Philadelphia Story* in New York. He's gone through a rough period and deserves a solid round of applause for his warm and lively accounting of himself.

ROGER: Tell me, just how weary are you?

ORSON: I refuse to bore you with a report on my health. I'll admit to being weary of dieting, but I'm continuing to lose weight, much to the delight of my doctor.

ROGER: Great. I always worry because you rarely level with me about your health. Tell me something that won't make me worry.

ORSON: John Gielgud called me the other day with a flattering proposal to appear with him in *The Tempest*.

ROGER: On the stage?

ORSON: No, in a film he's planning. He tells me that he's lined up British backers. He suggests I play Caliban to his Prospero. It's very tempting and flattering. I've wanted to film *The Tempest* since I saw Percy Stow's silent film a million years ago.

ROGER: So, it's not just idle talk?

ORSON: He's very serious, and, for a moment, I considered it. But, my God, to do the role justice requires great physical energy. Not only would it be exhausting, it would tie me up for months. I was touched by John's offer, but I'm going to turn him down.

ROGER: Too physically demanding.

ORSON: I could muster the energy, but right now, with all my film projects in limbo, I must spend what time I have left finding "end money" for what's already begun and solid backers for *Lear* and *Cradle*. I must remain optimistic that something will jell, *and as patient as a gentle stream and make a pastime of each weary step.*

ROGER: Yes, and keep reminding yourself *how poor are they that have not patience! What wound did ever heal but by degrees? Thou know'st we work by wit, and not by witchcraft; And wit depends on dilatory time.* You should give seminars on the subject of patience.

ORSON: You should be the one giving seminars on Shakespeare.

ROGER: No one is able to bring Will more vividly to life than you. As you wrote so well at nineteen in the introduction to our Shakespeare books—and I can quote you every line: "Shakespeare said everything. Brain to belly; every mood and minute of a man's season. His language is starlight and fireflies and the sun and moon. He wrote it with tears and blood and beer, and his words march like heart-beats. He speaks to everyone and we all claim him..." You must speak for him and make him real to today's generation. End of sermon. Are you making any headway with the French to retrieve your negative to *The Other Side of the Wind*?

ORSON: Not really. We continue to maintain an exasperatingly ineffectual correspondence, and they continue to stall in an attempt to nibble away at my endurance.

ROGER: Is work on *The Magic Show* more encouraging?

ORSON: That is a bright spot on the horizon. I'm about to wrap it up, actually. A few more camera set-ups and a slight bit more editing and that's it, except—

ROGER: Except what?

ORSON: Except, I'm tempted to add a new close: the teleportation of a human being along a fiber-optic cable from Los Angeles to New York.

ROGER: A new coast-to-coast fiber-optic hoax. I won't even ask how you plan to accomplish that sleight of eye, but keep me posted on your progress.

ORSON: I will, of course. A couple of networks are showing interest. After it's shown on television, it will go into theatrical release.

ROGER: It's over fifteen years since you began working on your magic show. The troubles you've encountered with this project alone would make for a great comi-tragic chapter.

ORSON: The only real troubles have been the perennial ones of finding money and time. But, it's been more a labor of love than one of necessity. My *Magic Show* troubles pale when I think of Okito, who was one of the greatest magicians. He invented one of my favorite tricks, the floating ball. He opened his act by plucking a duck from a cloth. Before making its entrance, the duck is secured in a bag between Okito's legs. At a command performance before the

Kings and Queens of Denmark and Holland, the duck somehow extricated its head out of the bag, and grabbed, with exceeding force, the very unsuspecting magician under his robe. Over the years, whenever I begin to believe I have troubles, I think of poor Okito. He's been on my mind a great deal in recent years. But, today, there's no duck under my djellabas, and the horizon is bright. I'm negotiating a new contract for a book. I really need to write volumes 1, 2, 3, 4, 5, and 6 of my memories to make enough money to finance my movies! I'm encouraged by the book contract, and confident that *The Magic Show* will be picked up. For the first time in years, I'm feeling hopeful that I'll be able to muster the money I need to complete many of my projects: *The Big Brass Ring, The Cradle Will Rock, The Dreamers,* and *Lear.* That reminds me, I want to send you a revised script of *The Dreamers.* I'll put it in the mail today.

ROGER: Wonderful. You're sounding optimistic.

ORSON: Yes, and a new reason for cautious optimism is a fellow who contacted me a few weeks ago, a professor of broadcasting at a university in Cincinnati. He claims he represents a wealthy character somewhere in the East, who is interested in investing in my work, and who chooses at this point to remain anonymous. A few days after his call, the professor came to Los Angeles and we had dinner. It appears there's substance to his talk and the only dilemma is deciding the first film to choose.

ROGER: What's your first choice?

ORSON: Either *The Dreamers* or *Lear.* I gave him a script of *The Dreamers* to take back with him. He called the next day and enthused over the script and asked

that I send him *Lear* as a second choice to present
to this mysterious advocate.

ROGER: Have you heard back?

ORSON: Yes, earlier this week, he called and was very excited
about both of them, but he thinks *Lear* is the
more marketable of the two. He's confident that
this man of mystery will agree. He ended the
conversation saying, "I can almost promise you,
you'll get your money."

ROGER: Oh, that's great news, Orson.

ORSON: There's no sustenance in promises and only the
barest of sustenance in hope. Working with the
French Ministry of Culture and an assortment of
television producers for so long has not proven to
be terribly profitable, as you know. The government
keeps slashing my budget and insisting on the
right of final cut, which is very disheartening.
That's why this flurry of interest is encouraging.

ROGER: Luck plays such a large part in life.

ORSON: Everything to do with an artistic career from
the fellow who eats live lizards for a living to
Michelangelo depends on an element of luck.
There's nobody who isn't beholden to luck.

ROGER: When do you hope to hear back?

ORSON: He's hoping to let me know within a week or
two.

ROGER: I read somewhere about a film that you're in that's
coming out soon. This is the first I've heard of it.
The review was kind, especially to you.

ORSON: *Someone to Love* is coming out soon. A young director friend of mine requested my presence in his picture.

ROGER: What's it about?

ORSON: My friend plays the role of a young film director with a slight case of angst, who invites a clutch of his friends to a theatre on Valentine's Day and commands each of them to define loneliness. I play the role of his mentor.

ROGER: Perfect typecasting.

ORSON: That's right. Much of the action takes place on the stage as a motley cast of characters in the director's personal and professional life flit about, attempting to answer his question. I remain in the back of the theatre and, from time to time, add an observation or two on the subject.

ROGER: Did you write your own lines, or were you reading them?

ORSON: I scripted much of my own part, but much was extemporaneous. There's one nice moment when, after being repeatedly pressed for a definition, I respond something like, "I have a terrible feeling that, because I am wearing a white beard and am sitting in the back of the theatre, you expect me to tell you the truth about something. These are the cheap seats, not Mount Sinai." The director persists and I eventually respond, "We're born alone, we live alone, we die alone. Only through our love and friendship can we create the illusion for the moment that we're not alone."

ROGER: How true.

ORSON: So then, when are you coming out to see me?

ROGER: I'll see if I can come out next month.

ORSON: I hope so. I'm feeling very mortal these days. I fear that, if you wait too long, your trip will be to deliver my eulogy.

ROGER: I think of you as immortal.

ORSON: Maybe in your eyes, but not in the eyes of my doctor. But, thank God, this shipwreck is too busy to be destroyed, let alone sink, and that *fortune brings in some boats that are not steered.* A phone is ringing. It's a money call I must take.

ROGER: Good luck and good night.

ORSON: Good night, Roger.

[Lights dim.]

Marlene Dietrich, George "Shorty" Chirello, and Orson between takes during the filming of Universal Pictures' *Follow the Boys.*

ACT THREE
SCENE NINE
OCTOBER 11, 1985
ORSON, ORSON, ORSON... AFTER LIFE'S
FITFUL FEVER, SLEEP WELL

Interior of Roger and Orson's libraries, 10:00 a.m. Roger picks up telephone receiver and dials Orson. The telephone rings three times in Orson's dark library with no response, which activates his answering system.

ORSON: [Recorded message] Please leave a message. Orson.

ROGER: Orson, was your money call fruitful? I thought I'd push my visit from next month to next week. Call me and let me know if next week is good for you. You're so right; we can no longer kid ourselves that we are immortal.

Roger hangs up the phone and turns on a radio on his desk. After absorbing the first line of the newscast, Roger slumps in his chair, lowers his head, and cups his face as he continues to listen.

Announcer: This just in, Orson Welles, the Hollywood "boy wonder" who created the film classic *Citizen Kane*, scared tens of thousands of Americans with a realistic radio report of a Martian invasion of New Jersey and changed the face of film and theater with his daring new ideas, died yesterday in Los Angeles, apparently of a heart attack. He was 70 years old and lived in Los Angeles, California and Las Vegas, Nevada.

Despite the feeling of many that his career—which evoked almost constant controversy over its 50 years—was one of largely unfulfilled promise, Welles eventually won the respect of his colleagues. He received the Lifetime Achievement Award of the American Film Institute in 1975, and last year the Directors Guild of America gave him its highest honor, the D. W. Griffith Award.

An assistant coroner in Los Angeles, Donald Messerle, said Welles's death "appears to be natural in origin." He had been under treatment for diabetes as well as a heart ailment, his physician reported. Welles's body was found by his chauffeur.

In film, his innovations in deep-focus technology and his use of theater aesthetics—long takes without close-ups, making the viewer's eye search the screen as if it were a stage—created a new vocabulary for the cinema.

By age 24, he was already being described by the press as a has-been—a cliché that would dog him all his life. But at that very moment Welles was creating *Citizen Kane*, generally considered one of the best motion pictures ever made. This scenario was repeated several times. His second film, *The Magnificent Ambersons*, was poorly received, but is now also regarded as a classic.

His life was a series of adventures whose details are fuzzy, in part because he was a bit of a fabulist, delighting in pulling the legs of listeners.

The film and television writer Stephen Farber commented: "Looking back over American movie history—a history of wrecked careers—you begin to see that the critics have a lot to answer for. The classic victim is Orson Welles."

He was the legendary sort of figure upon whom old anecdotes are rehung. Herman J. Mankiewicz, for example, was to have said of Welles, "There, but for the grace of God, goes God."

Welles inspired harsh criticism, yet most people felt that even his most unsuccessful, most self-indulgent works all had some feature, some turn that was memorable. There were no dissenters when, at the dedication of a Theater Hall of Fame in New York in 1972, his name was among the first to be chosen.

Roger takes his hands away from his face and turns the radio off. He sits immobile for several seconds, stands, and with tears in his eyes, he begins to pace.

ROGER: Orson, Orson, Orson... *After life's fitful fever he sleeps well.*

Treason has done his worst; nor steel, nor poison, Malice domestic, foreign levy, nothing Can touch him further.

[Lights dim.]

THE CURTAIN COMES DOWN

THE END

THE FOREMOST NAME IN AMERICAN
ESTHETIC LIFE TODAY

"It turns out that there are two
ways of doing Shakespeare, the
old way and the good way."
—ROBERT BENCHLEY,
THE NEW YORKER

"How young I once was."

EPILOGUE

For more than a half century, the world constantly wanted something from Orson: his talent, his celebrity, his time. My grandfather wanted nothing from Orson save his success and happiness.

Now that both have been gone for more than two decades, I'm reminded of Orson's powerful words celebrating the medieval French Cathedral at Chartres and man, in his film *F for Fake*:

> All that's left, most artists seem to feel these days, is man. Naked, poor, forked radish. There aren't any celebrations. Ours, the scientists keep telling us, is a universe which is disposable....Our works in stone, in paint, in print are spared, some of them for a few decades, or a millennium or two, but everything must fall in war or wear away into the ultimate and universal ash: the triumphs and the frauds, the treasures and the fakes. A fact of life—we're going to die. 'Be of good heart,' cry the dead artists out of the living past. Our songs will all be silenced, but what of it? Go on singing. Maybe a man's name doesn't matter all that much.

Orson and Roger's voices are now silenced, but, thankfully, their music remains.

"'Be of good heart,' cry the dead artists out of the living past. Our songs will all be silenced—but what of it? Go on singing."

ACKNOWLEDGMENTS

There are not a few people that I wish to thank for their assistance in transforming the idea of *Orson Welles and Roger Hill: A Friendship in Three Acts* into a reality. My foremost gratitude is to the book's principal protagonists for the indelible footprints they left on one another's hearts—and mine—captured in their conversations and correspondence.

Jonathan Rosenbaum, film critic and historian, deserves special thanks for his steadfast support of *Friendship*. After completing a first draft, I inquired if he would be interested in reading the manuscript, which at the time had a working title of *Standing in a Hammock*. Jonathan was interested, and after reading it, he was generous in his evaluation, but he found the title wanting, suggesting instead, a far stronger one that captures the essence of the narrative, *Orson Welles and Roger Hill: A Friendship in Four Acts*. With his permission, I appropriated it, ultimately changing "Four Acts" to "Three."

I applaud Simon Callow for his warm support of *Friendship* and his treasured counsel. I am grateful to Orson's co-author of *This is Orson Welles* and fellow director, Peter Bogdanovich, for his enthusiastic response to the book.

I am indebted to Tom Leiser for his insightful vetting of the play. Jim Saxon's contribution was not insignificant. After reading the original four acts he suggested I consider compressing them into three. "I can't help thinking that, like a great sculpture, the play only needs a little chipping away to reveal the beauty and symmetry that was there all along." Jim was right, and it is my hope the reader will agree that the final result brings to light *Friendship*'s "beauty and symmetry."

I'm appreciative of Richard Feinberg ably demonstrating that proofreading is an invaluable art. Valerie Thompson's deft design is an important fillip in capturing Orson and Roger's music. BearManor Media's Sandra Grabman's assistance and kindness is much appreciated.

To gain a deeper perspective of Orson's personal and professional life, I spent valuable hours at the Special Collections Library at the University of Michigan in Ann Arbor that houses an extensive collection of Wellesiana. Peggy Daub and Kate Hutchens could not have been more accommodating. I extend my thanks as well to Isabel Planton at the Lilly Library, Indiana University (home to another superlative Welles collection). Praise to Martha Hansen, Reference Librarian/ Network Administrator at the Woodstock (IL) Public Library for keeping the Todd School for Boys flame alive in the library's files and on the Internet.

I owe a special tribute to Patrick McGilligan, author of *George Cukor: A Double Life* and *Alfred Hitchcock: A Life in Darkness and Light*, for directing me to BearManor Media. Just as Orson was an independent film director and producer, Ben Ohmart is the independent publisher of BearManor Media. Orson and Skipper would undoubtedly be delighted that *Friendship* is issued by such a sympathetic publishing house. I certainly am.

My deepest appreciation is reserved for Shirley, my gimlet-eyed editor and superlative wife of 43 years, who is quick to discover and recast an errant phrase, and quicker to forgive and cosset an errant husband.

T.T.
BARRINGTON HILLS, ILLINOIS
MARCH, 2013

CREDITS

The author is grateful for permission to reprint an excerpt from
ORSON WELLES by Barbara Leaming, Copyright © 1983, 1985
by Barbara Leaming

THE FOLLOWING ILLUSTRATIONS APPEAR
BY THE GENEROUS PERMISSION OF:

PAGE 21. Orson Welles & Oja Kodar Papers, Special Collections
Library, University of Michigan

PAGE 24. Florence Dauman ©

PAGE 109. Woodstock Public Library (IL)

PAGE 125. Orson Welles & Oja Kodar Papers, Special Collections
Library, University of Michigan

PAGE 173. Orson Welles & Oja Kodar Papers, Special Collections
Library, University of Michigan

PAGE 210. Orson Welles & Oja Kodar Papers, Special Collections
Library, University of Michigan

PAGE 238. Bancroft Library, UC Berkeley

PAGE 288. Enrico Nocera, Pubblicita

PAGE 302. Nicolas Tikhomiroff, Magnum Photos ©

ALL OTHER IMAGES ARE FROM THE AUTHOR'S PRIVATE COLLECTION.

INDEX

ABOUT THE AUTHOR

Photograph by Shirley Tarbox

TODD TARBOX was born in Chicago, Illinois, in 1944, and attended the Todd School for Boys until it closed. He is the author of *See the World, Imagine*, and co-editor with his wife of *Footprints of Young Explorers*. He is working on a book about a childhood friend who possessed inestimable talent, charisma, and promise—valedictorian of his suburban Milwaukee high school, a student athlete at Yale, class secretary, All-Ivy linebacker—and the impact of his death in Hong Kong a month after graduating. Tarbox lives in Barrington Hills, Illinois.